'In this intriguing book Alex Durig vigorou[s] mystical – borderland between autism and and creative challenge to conventional thi arouse controversy while it broadens persp

'Alex Durig presents a clear, alternative paradigm to professionals, parents, and adults who "don't get" autism. Durig is a seminal thinker. In explaining autistic perception and behavior, his insight is as significant a contribution to understanding human thought and behavior as the writings and teachings of L.S. Vygotsky, A.R. Luria, Herb Lovett, Tony Attwood and Deirdre V. Lovecky. Using a unique approach, Durig emphasizes the spectral nature of autism. He rejects the autism industry's misdirected medical/scientific stereotypic views about autism, approaches that fundamentally disparage and disrespect human differences. Durig is critical of "expert" characterizations wedded to terms implying the *fix-it/cure it* baggage of moralistic disapprobation such as *disease, disorder, deficits, dysfunctional, and disabled.*

For professionals and lay readers alike, Durig explains why perceiving autistic individuals through the lens of "normalization" does not work. He clearly explains why medical, scientific, and education industry efforts to squeeze individuals on the spectrum into diagnostic boxes (that leak!) have accounted for documented, continued failed efforts to improve the quality of life of their clients/patients/students/children. By presenting autism as a *different mental process* of meaningfully perceiving the world, Durig proposes a model of individual human differences based upon two critical constructs: *Social Thinking and Computer Thinking.* Rather than using language and terms that have historically distorted experts' characterizations of autism, he presents the reader with a clear, *intuitively correct visual chart model* designed to enlighten the reader, and, for the first time, successfully explain human differences in perception and behavior in humanistic, empathetic terms. For anyone involved with autistic spectrum issues, Durig's book is a "must read".'

— *Roger N. Meyer,*
author of Asperger Syndrome Employment Workbook

of related interest

The Development of Autism
A Self-Regulatory Perspective
Thomas L. Whitman
ISBN 978 1 84310 735 4

Asperger's Syndrome
A Guide for Parents and Professionals
Tony Attwood
Foreword by Lorna Wing
ISBN 978 1 85302 577 8

Freaks, Geeks and Asperger Syndrome
A User Guide to Adolescence
Luke Jackson
Foreword by Tony Attwood
ISBN 978 1 84310 098 0

Understanding Autism Spectrum Disorders
Frequently Asked Questions
Diane Yapko
ISBN 978 1 84310 756 9

How To Understand Autism – The Easy Way

Alex Durig

Jessica Kingsley Publishers
London and Philadelphia

First published in 2005
by Jessica Kingsley Publishers
116 Pentonville Road
London N1 9JB, UK
and
400 Market Street, Suite 400
Philadelphia, PA 19106, USA

www.jkp.com

Library of Congress Cataloging in Publication Data

Durig, Alexander, 1959-
    How to understand autism - the easy way / Alexander Durig.
        p. cm.
    Includes index.
    ISBN 1-84310-791-0 (pbk.)
    1. Autism--Popular works. I. Title.
    RC553.A88D873 2005
    616.85'882--dc22

                                                    2004015476

British Library Cataloguing in Publication Data

A CIP catalogue record for this book is available from the British Library

ISBN 978 1 84310 791 0

For Lydia

Acknowledgements

The author would like to thank the following people, without whom the book in its present form would not exist: my mother, Delma Durig, who insisted on buying me a new desk when I told her I wanted to write this book; my brother, Albert Durig, who advised me at every stage from the beginning to making editing suggestions on the final drafts; my literary agents, Mike and Susan Farris, who know so much about writing and publishing, for sharing with me their editing suggestions, patience, professionalism, and confidence; my son, Nick Durig, for time and advice in final stages of the project.

Lastly, I want to thank my daughter, Lydia Durig, for her special role in the development of this project: it is not an exaggeration to say that without her influence the sequence of events that led to the development of this book would not have taken place.

Contents

Introduction

It was a hot, muggy afternoon in downtown Cincinnati, Ohio. I believe it was August of 1991. I was lucky to have a chance to share my new ideas about perception with a very distinguished senior professor. We had a few minutes for lunch and I took advantage of the time away from our professional meetings to talk to him about my dissertation: a new way of understanding perception.

Soon the old professor began banging on the table. Dishes and silverware clanged loudly with each pounding of his fist. People in the restaurant turned to look at us. He was a nationally recognized professor at a major university – the chair of the number one department in his field. I was just a graduate student at the time.

"Not one person in the entire nation will ever care about any of these ideas! Not one person! These ideas are completely meaningless! Your claims about perception have no foundation in any concepts accepted in modern science! Who do you think you are?!"

By this time the restaurant had become completely quiet and everyone was staring at us. I was completely humiliated. And then it dawned on me. If he was so right and I was so wrong, why was he becoming so upset?

★ ★ ★

The history of human progress is the story of new discoveries appearing, seemingly out of nowhere, to challenge an existing worldview. Take, for example, Albert Einstein suggesting that everything in our universe exists relative to the speed of light. Once a new worldview is accepted we take it for granted as normal. But, before his discovery was announced, no one had a clue it was on the way. Before even Einstein could develop and present his work, he had to believe it was possible to find a new way of looking at an old mystery. Without the conviction that being open-minded was key he would not have been able to accomplish his work.

The purpose of this book is to share a new way of looking at the mystery of autism. Will you, too, be open-minded as you begin reading this book?

The fact is that in all of modern science there is yet to appear any means of understanding autism. In spite of years of research there is absolutely no singular explanation that allows us to apprehend why people with autism behave the way they do. We are still asking the same questions.

- "Why do people with autism evidence repetitive, persevering behaviors?"
- "Why do savants have their unbelievable talents?"
- "Why do some autistic people have trouble recognizing themselves in a mirror?"
- "What is the best way to initiate communication with an autistic person?"
- "As a teacher, what should I do if an autistic child becomes upset at school?"
- "I have a friend who says he is 'a little bit' autistic – is that possible?"

We are going to tackle these questions. How would it make you feel if you could find an easy way of understanding autism that would allow you to begin answering these questions? That is what we will be doing in this book.

Going beyond normal science

We hear that scientists continue to make gains in autism research. They can describe autism in more and more detail. They can recognize autistic perception and behavior in finer and finer gradations of detail. But, they still cannot tell us how to understand autistic perception, and why autistic perception leads to autistic behaviors such as the tendency toward repetitive, persevering actions. Without that kind of understanding parents and teachers interested in autism are left with increasing levels of frustration and alienation. It is difficult to have a philosophy of parenting or teaching without having any real understanding of the child with autism.

This book seeks to fill that gap by providing a meaningful understanding of autistic perception and behavior. In this book we will examine a logical way of addressing human perception. You will see something you've never seen before: a simple way of understanding human perception. *As soon as you see it you will be amazed by how easy it is!*

The power of this book rests on the old truism that the best ideas are the simplest ideas. You do not need a Ph.D. to understand this book. You just need an open mind. You do not need to understand psychology or brain neuroscience to understand this book. You just need a desire to understand autism. I took a Ph.D. in the social psychology of perception. Then I developed my dissertation on perception to embrace a new understanding of autism. The ideas in this book are drawn from psychology, sociology, symbolic interactionism, sociolinguistics, semantics, logic, and philosophy. The goal is to communicate these ideas in plain language.

Of course, as soon as I discovered a new way of under-standing autism I was notified repeatedly by "normal profes-sors" that it was not "normal science." It existed outside of modern psychology completely. Therefore I knew there was little chance of it being accepted anytime soon within that world. So, I dedicated the years following the publication of my first book, *Autism and the Crisis of Meaning*, to presenting these ideas in plain English to real people in the real world. I wanted to be able to explain these ideas to anyone. As a college professor living in San Diego, California, I began taking advantage of every opportunity available to speak to the general public about autism.

One of the great highlights from this episode in my life was meeting Bernard Rimland, perhaps the world's foremost autism expert. For decades in psychology it was considered standard practice to blame the appearance of autism on the mother of the child. It was the Freudian approach to autism. Can you imagine the experience of parents who were blamed by professionals for their child being autistic?

This changed when a book titled *Infantile Autism: The Syndrome and Its Implications for a Neural Theory of Behavior* was published in 1964. Bernard Rimland wrote the book that changed the tide from a worldview that blamed autism on refrigerator mothers, to a worldview in which autism came to be understood as a brain-based congenital condition. Rimland proceeded to pioneer the neurological approach to autism, which has become a diverse field of inquiry into the biochemi-cal underpinnings of autistic perception. For example, this line of research analyzes how allergens and toxins can affect the brain and central nervous system to present autistic perception and behavior. Rimland's insistence on creative approaches to autism has been an inspiration to me.

Since the early 1990s I have shared the ideas you will be reading about in this book with people in all walks of life, from children to the elderly, from parents of children with autism to experts in the world of autism. Interestingly, it's the real people in the real world with the greatest personal investment in the world of autism that have been the first to applaud these insights. Whether it is the mother who receives meaningful advice on how to teach social etiquette to her son, or the daughter receiving new insight on the mysterious behavior of her father, whenever I talk to interested people they often go away feeling a little less crazy.

Once, I met a former mayor of a California city who, after listening to me give a public lecture, invited me to his home to meet his wife and receive a book as a gift. He told me I was the first person who had been able to help him understand his son. His son was in his fifties at that time. Although his son had never been diagnosable in any formal sense, his son had never been quite normal either. When he heard me discussing the concept of slight autism, he felt I was talking about his son.

On the other hand, professionals whose careers are invested in traditional science have, at times, treated me like I must be crazy. Negative responses seem to be based in the commitment to find a cure for autism. In other words, many people feel that since my ideas lead to no obvious cure or drug for autism, then I must not be on the right track. But, this book presents real understanding and suggests that no miracle cure or drug will mysteriously arise from our current state of ignorance.

In this book, *How To Understand Autism – The Easy Way*, you will find a host of ideas and insights that will allow you to get a handle on the phenomenon of autism. We will attain a degree of objectivity that far outstrips the medieval jabberwocky that assumes an autistic person is broken and needs to be fixed, sick and needs to be cured, strange and needs to be made normal.

Once you understand autism, you will agree that the single biggest problem we have suffered in the world of autism is a lack of understanding.

You will see that autism professionals are tacitly committed to making autistic children behave normally. But, it's also a source of tremendous frustration for the professionals themselves. If professionals assume we need to engage a program for normalizing the autistic child, and if our progress is measured in the degree to which each child is normalized, then we are teaching an autistic child from a normal point of view. That might not necessarily be the best approach to educating an autistic child.

Regardless of whether or not a cure is found, everyone will benefit from a logical and empathetic understanding of autism. This book is not dedicated to helping autistic people become normal. It is dedicated to helping normal people understand autism. *Talk to any parent of an autistic child and they will tell you that no one understands autism.*

For many years autism professionals have chosen to focus on the normalization, or cure, of autism as the primary goal of their work. There are many books describing autism and proposing means of conditioning normal behaviors, but there has been no comparable work in support of understanding autism. Underneath most of the autism literature lies a commitment to normalcy.[1] There is a creeping assumption that autism is undesirable – a mere curiosity of life.

Fortunately, more and more autobiographical works by people with strong autistic perception have allowed readers to go farther than simple advocacy of autism and to begin to see the world through the eyes of a person with autism. Take, for example, the writings of Donna Williams. Such works have helped us to go beyond our treatment of autism as a curiosity. We need to be able to see the world through the eyes of a person who has autism. We need to reexamine our assumptions of normalcy, because implicit in our assumptions of normalcy lies hidden the idea that the autistic person is an inferior person.

It's not hard to see how parents of children with autism can end up feeling vexed. There is no consensus regarding our understanding of autism, and research in the neurological approach indicates there are actually many different ways of becoming autistic. It's no wonder so much weight and attention has been given to the genetic approach for a cure. But since there are many ways to become autistic and many kinds of autistic perception, even if we were able to engineer our perception scientifically we would still be left with the question "How do we define normal and who gets to decide?"

In other words, in this book you will discover that the full range of autistic perception is as vast as the number of channels on digital cable. I don't think we are likely to decide on one kind of normal perception that we wish engineered into our children any more than we are likely to decide on one cable television channel we will all want to watch. Furthermore, in this book we will examine how autism is actually a window on the mind itself. It's possible that autistic perception may actually underlie a number of other human conditions that are not currently associated with autism, such as Alzheimer's disease and various types of so-called mental illness.

Autistic perception is that important and it is that varied. We will not sweep it under the rug by finding a cure for autism tomorrow. For these reasons, I will suggest that autistic perception is actually one of the most important aspects of our lives as social creatures, and it is something that ought to be under-stood and paid attention to always.

Another important thing to keep in mind is that the appearance of autism transcends all demographic categories with consistency. We are all implicated in this universal aspect of the human mind. Autism knows no boundaries whatsoever. Anybody anywhere can have a child who is eventually diag-nosed as autistic. That is why the endeavor to understand autism in a practical way is an important social issue.

Becoming autism-friendly

In essence what we will be doing is assuming that there are logical ways of thinking wired into the brain. Modern science has no way of saying this. Scientists are committed to the idea that logic is not wired into the human brain.

In contemporary science, logic is conceptualized as formal logic, which is the basis for computers and robots. But, people are not computers and robots, so scientists believe logic can't be wired into the brain. In academic terms, to claim that logic is wired into the brain is tantamount to committing scientific heresy. In other words, this book represents a departure from normal science!

However, the book is based on two fundamental commit-ments:

1.   the ability to think logically is wired into the brain

2.   every human being deserves trust, respect, safety, and comfort.

To be able to understand the way each of us is wired up for logical thinking is the key to understanding the mind and per-ception. This will help us to begin understanding autism. To be able to give each person trust, respect, safety, and comfort is the key to understanding sophisticated relationships and good communication. This will lead us toward becoming autism-friendly.

To become autism-friendly means that the normal world of business and professional activities can begin to find ways to help autistic people and their families to be more comfortable when in need of their services. This would imply that businesses and professionals would offer special services for families of autism. We will be discussing ways to be autism-friendly later on in this book.

The asset approach: Beyond medicalization and the deficit approach

So, how do we define autism? We know that autism represents challenges in social life. People with autism have issues with social interaction. Basically we have descriptions of what autistic people do. However, we have no explanations for why autistic people do what they do. Psychology tells us children diagnosed with autism are said to have impaired communication, little or no imaginary play, trouble with social interaction, and a predilection for repetitive, persevering behavior.

But this book stands outside of traditional definitions and treatments for children with autism. Instead of evaluating people with autism in terms of their deficits, we ought to begin appreciating them for their assets as well. Any one of us would fall short of the mark if we were described in terms of our deficits. We need to understand that a deficit approach is the automatic result of the medicalization of autism.

For example, the medical model that is used as the basis of psychology and neuroscience is not capable of giving us insight or understanding into the perception and behaviors of autism. When we medicalize autism we assume we have found the disease, labeled it, and must now set out to look for a cure.

But, this approach has slighted the importance of understanding, appreciating, and facing autism.

Psychiatrists have amassed a book called the *Diagnostic and Statistical Manual of Mental Disorders* (DSM). It is the bible of mental disorders and mental illnesses. Every name and label that can be officially used by a psychologist or psychiatrist is in the DSM. Curiously, the DSM gets bigger every time a new version is published. I used to joke with my students that one day we will all be in the DSM.

But the fact that the DSM exists as a diagnostic reference point implies that the reference point itself is normalcy. Either you are in the DSM or you are normal. Generally, people don't place much credence in the word "normal." But I use the term here because it seems to be a good place to locate the people who have been in charge of judging and evaluating and describing autism.

To this extent, the world of normal people and the world of autistic people have existed as diametrically opposed to one another. This is the deficit approach. Autism is understood in terms of its shortcomings. Autism and normalcy have been defined as mutually exclusive. That is, a human being is either in one world or the other. But one of the themes of this book will be to address this assumption of normalcy in a new way. What if these two worlds are not so mutually exclusive after all? Is it in fact possible that each world is intimately related with the other? This is the beginning of an asset approach to autism.

The biggest problem confronting autistic people is the general level of ignorance about autistic perception that has existed in the normal world. Normal people need to learn how to understand autism in order to communicate with autistic people more efficiently and graciously. Normal people, especially business people and professionals, need to learn how to understand autism in order to help people with autism to feel as safe and comfortable as possible.

Many people will be surprised when we examine the notion that autistic people not only have their own kind of meaningful experience, but also their own experience of mental health. But the concept of mental health was created in the normal world and applied automatically to normal people. It is not surprising that we never thought to apply it to autistic people as well.

Another theme of this book is that autism does not exist in a few distinct forms. The official line of psychology has told us that a person either has autism, high-functioning autism, a pervasive developmental disorder (which is a way of saying they don't fit into the first two categories but they are still not quite normal), or they have Asperger's syndrome. The problem is that psychology has no way of explaining the relation between these categories. In recent years psychologists have begun to admit there is actually a wide range of autistic perception, but the DSM classification system itself defies the ability to describe a smooth continuum of autistic perceptions.

What is the red thread that runs throughout the range of autistic perceptions? And if there is a range of autistic perceptions, can we define autistic perception in terms of a sliding scale instead of a few labels we use to pigeonhole everyone? In this book we will consider the notion that there is actually a range, or continuum, of autistic perception that takes many forms. We will even see that it is possible to imagine a person who favors autistic perception but is not diagnosably autistic. We will refer to these people as slightly autistic. We will also see how easy it is to describe this range of autistic perception using a simple model of social and computer thinking.

How To Understand Autism – The Easy Way will cover the following issues:

- a simple model for understanding autism
- the six functions of perception
- how the model goes beyond modern science to explain autistic behaviors that have been previously unexplained
- how we are all autistic to one extent or another
- three keys to enabling communication with autistic people
- the practical side of understanding autism: how insight and understanding yields many tips for teaching and interacting with autistic people.

Autistic meaning, mind, and self

The field of social science is based in the notion that a person's behavior is grounded in meaning. That is, a person's meaningful perception of the world enables and supports that person's behavior. But nowhere in social science do we find any explanation for how the brain perpetually organizes its meaningful perception of the world. In order to understand autism we have to understand meaning. Likewise, as soon as we understand how the brain organizes its meaningful perception of the world, we will be able to entertain the notion that autism is a different kind of meaningful perception.

Autism has long been misunderstood in modern science as a state of mind devoid of meaning. It has also been described as a state of mind with no self. But we will assume the opposite. We will engage a way of understanding autism that allows for autistic people to have their own experience of meaning and self. Any parent of a child diagnosed with autism will tell you that they already knew this. It is curious that it has taken the world so long to catch up to this.

However, as soon as we have this new way of understanding autism before us, we will then be able to begin making recommendations for how to communicate more effectively with people who have autism. Time and again normal people in the normal world try to impose their own normal perceptions and behaviors on autistic people and then stand back and wonder why they have so little success. But once we have a handle on how to understand autism we will also have gained tremendous insights into the things we should and should not do when interacting with autistic people.

Perhaps the single greatest benefit of this way of truly understanding autism is that we begin by assuming that each autistic child has their own meaningful experience, their own sense of self, and therefore their own experience of mental health. It is probably the greatest mistake of our misunderstanding of autism that we have robbed autistic people of the credit for having their own meaningful experience. I say robbed because the foundation of any human interaction rests on meaning. And when we say that someone is not capable of experiencing a meaningful perception of the world, then we are saying that they are not really human.

We will see how autism can be understood as a different kind of meaningful perception. We will see how to understand the way this meaningful perception is formulated. We will also see that there is possibly a range of autistic perceptions stemming from the strongest cases of autism to the slightest. And we will even consider how the logic of autistic perception can be seen throughout the social structures of the normal world.

By the end of this book we will have come face to face with the notion that autism and the normal world are actually inseparable. We will be able to recognize that autistic perception is part and parcel of all human perception.

We are now embarking on a new way of understanding autism. And we shouldn't be too surprised if we also have found a new way of understanding ourselves. It's time for the normal world to embrace autism as an important legacy of the human experience. To understand autism is to discover new meaning in a world that tends to take for granted that it knows as much as it can know. Autism presents us all with a challenge. It's time for us to reexamine ourselves and the way we perceive the world. It's time for us to understand autism.

Note

1. The words *normal* and *normalcy* are used throughout this book extensively. What is normal? Does anyone really believe there is such a thing as a normal person? Probably not. Most people nowadays view human beings as diverse creatures each with a unique profile of characteristics. So, the use of these words *normal* and *normalcy* is only intended from the most practical standpoint. At the same time, the challenge to families and teachers of autistic children is based on the simple idea that however the concept of *normal* is used, it is always employed to the exclusion of autistic children. In other words, whatever the normal world is, it has never included autistic children. This work promotes an integration of the worlds of normalcy and autism. We should be able to look forward to a day when everyone sees the normal world as a place that includes all of our children, some of whom may be labeled as autistic. One day, the truest meaning of respect for diversity will include people's different styles of perception. Our normalcy will be our diversity.

Chapter One

Social Thinking and Computer Thinking

Forget about everything you know for a moment. Just open your mind and consider this.

There are three kinds of thinking wired into the human brain. There is social thinking. There is computer thinking. And there is creative thinking. Let's assume that the creative thinking is wired into both the social thinking and the computer thinking. That means we can be creative with our social thinking and we can be creative with our computer thinking.

Now then, let's just focus on the social and the computer for the time being in order to keep things simple. Let's imagine that there is a normal person standing in front of us. Imagine that this normal person has equal amounts of social and computer thinking. We can draw a picture of this (see Figure 1.1).

This picture represents the range of human ability, from the lowest possible social thinking to the highest, and from the lowest possible computer thinking to the highest. And we imagine that normal people have equal amounts of social thinking and computer thinking wired into their brain. We place the levels of social and computer in the middle of the picture. This way, we can imagine that this normal person has average amounts of social and computer thinking.

Now, let's take the level of social thinking and drop it dramatically (see Figure 1.2). What kind of person is this?

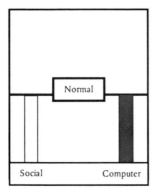

Figure 1.1 Normal perception

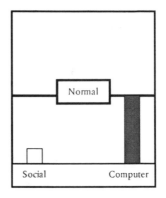

Figure 1.2 Autistic perception

This person will more than likely be diagnosed as autistic. This person might have the same amount of computer thinking as a normal person, but social thinking is far lower, so they will have marked problems with social life. Because they will have much more of a problem doing social life than a normal person, they will be recognized as socially challenged.

Since this person is higher on the computer thinking, all of the activities we humans perform that require social thinking will tend to elude this person. So, we have created a category for these people. We say they are autistic. At times, this person may tend to act more like a computer or a robot than a person.

Think about it this way for a moment. A computer calculates 2 + 2 = 4, 2 + 2 = 4, 2 + 2 = 4, it's always the same. The computer will never calculate 2 + 2 = 5, or 2 + 2 = 3. The computer will calculate 2 + 2 = 4 over and over and over, again and again and again, with perfect precision and predictability.

People with autism tend to do the same things over and over and over again. It often annoys and bewilders the normal people around them. But, you can already see that if your social is far lower than your computer, then your computer thinking will anchor you in a perception of the world that tends to repeat itself over and over again, regardless of what anyone else thinks! In fact, if your computer is higher than your social, your perception is anchored in repetitive patterns, and you can't help it!

One of the first mistakes normal people make when they view an autistic person is to assume that they must try to get the autistic person to stop their persevering repetitive motions. But it is not necessarily wise crudely to assume that we have to get that person to stop, because the fact is that he just can't help it. What we need is more understanding of that person. And now that we have this simple picture of the social and the computer, we can already begin to get a handle on why autistic people engage repetitive, persevering motions.

Did you know that in all of psychology there is no explanation for why autistic people engage repetitive, persevering behaviors? This is seen as one of the greatest mysteries of autism. But psychology can't explain it because psychology treats perception as one thing. The beauty of these pictures is that we are looking at perception as something that is made up of both social and computer thinking, as well as the creative thinking that is inside of each. And in these simple pictures we can imagine that the levels of the social thinking and computer thinking are independent of each other.

At this point, the fascination begins to take shape. Is it possible for us to continue playing with these levels of social and computer thinking? What kind of people may we describe as we keep drawing different levels of each? What kind of person is this? (See Figure 1.3.)

This person has normal computer, but the social thinking is noticeably higher than the autistic person in the last picture. I would suggest that this person stands a good chance of being labeled as high-functioning autistic. Make sense?

We have the same issues before us, but since the social is higher, this person will be more efficient in social life than the autistic person in Figure 1.2. But, this person will still have an almost gravitational pull away from the social because the computer thinking is stronger. We will still see a marked tendency toward repetitive behavior. But we will also see a marked improvement in this person's ability to do social life.

This is becoming like a game. Are you ready for another picture? What kind of person is this? Think about it for a minute (see Figure 1.4).

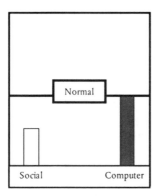

Figure 1.3 High-functioning autistic

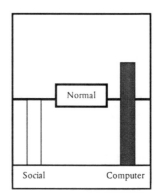

Figure 1.4 Asperger's syndrome

Things are quickly starting to get interesting here. This person has normal social thinking. So, we would expect them to be able to do social life in a fairly normal way. But, the computer thinking is quite a bit higher than normal. Would this create a condition similar to the high-functioning autism in the last picture? Would this person have an almost magnetic pull away from the social, even though they are capable of presenting themselves as fairly normal in social life? Would this person have a marked tendency toward repetitive motions of one kind or another?

I think the answer to these questions is "Yes." In fact, there is a chance this person would be diagnosed with Asperger's syndrome. Asperger's is the super high-functioning autistic condition that professionals have struggled to associate with autism. By the way, there is also a chance this person will escape any diagnosis at all.

Psychologists have wanted to associate Asperger's syndrome with autism because both labels address obvious challenges in performing normal social behavior. Yet they have struggled with it because they have no basis for understanding what links it all together. It becomes another labeled category of behavior that is described but not understood. But, this idea of the social and the computer thinking, and these pictures we are considering, allow us to begin to see that autistic perception actually exists in a full range of appearances.

Now, if the social was above normal and the computer was slightly higher still, this person would be slightly autistic, but might be able to mask it and pass as normal for the most part. The concept of slight autism is presented in this book to describe any perception that is slightly higher on the computer thinking than the social thinking. This ratio of slightly higher computer to social thinking could exist anywhere on the continuum. For example, they could both be below normal with the computer slightly higher. Or they could both be above normal with the computer slightly higher (see Figure 1.5).

This slightly autistic perception yields behavior that is recognizable as autistic while not diagnosable as a form of autism in existing clinical terms. Such a perception would present

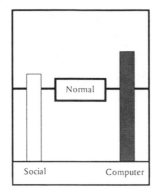

Figure 1.5 Slightly autistic with high levels of social and computer thinking

autistic perceptions and behaviors that slightly overshadow a recognizable set of social skills. There is a very good chance that you are in this category yourself or you know somebody who is! I believe this idea of being slightly autistic applies to many, many people. *Whenever the computer is favored over the social, we will have some kind of perception that is essentially autistic in its characteristics.*

What kind of person is this in Figure 1.6?

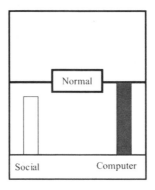

Figure 1.6 Slightly autistic with possible diagnosis of pervasive developmental disorder

This person is also slightly autistic. They would possibly be labeled as having a pervasive developmental disorder. In other words, a psychologist might say that this child is not exactly autistic or high-functioning autistic, or a candidate for Asperger's syndrome. They would announce that this child seems to have a pervasive developmental disorder. This child is definitely not completely normal, but at the same time, definitely not completely autistic. The person is fairly normal, but has some distinct social issues.

Note that the label pervasive developmental disorder serves to categorize people who do not fit into any other label! The label and the category are meaningless because it was obviously made up to encompass children that were not easily diagnosable as either autistic or high-functioning autistic. It's a case of devising a category and a label for the DSM that is not based on clear understanding of the phenomenon at hand so much as on the need to have a category for the children that do not fit neatly into any other category.

Let's consider a few more quick examples. Who might be reflected in Figure 1.7?

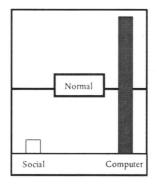

Figure 1.7 Autistic savant

I would suggest this might begin to describe an autistic savant, like Dustin Hoffman portrayed in *Rain Man*. At least in some respects, this person's computer is way, way higher than anyone else's, while at the same time the social seems to be too low to allow for anything resembling normal social life. Indeed, savants are often capable of computational genius that far exceeds anything usually seen in normal life.

With one model using both social and computer thinking we have been able to address a wide range of human perception that can be characterized as autistic. With this model we can run a red thread through all the phenomena that can be qualified as autistic perception. Now let's turn the tables and consider some pictures where the social thinking is higher than the computer thinking. What kind of person might be described in Figure 1.8?

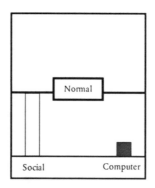

Figure 1.8 Severe learning difficulties

This person would probably be labeled as having "severe learning difficulties". Being normal on the social thinking would make them a loving person. But, the computer is so low that they would have trouble computing appropriate behavior. They would also be extremely slow to learn, generally speaking.

What about the person in Figure 1.9?

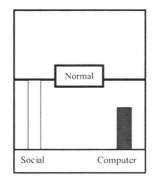

Figure 1.9 Down's syndrome

This person would likely be labeled as having "moderate learning difficulties," or perhaps it would describe someone with Down's syndrome. Very social, but slow to learn. In some sense Down's syndrome can be thought of as the opposite of autism. Likewise, people with varying levels of mental retardation can also be loving and affectionate. They can be very sociable.

And what about the person in Figure 1.10?

This person would probably be a politician, a successful businessperson, or a successful actor; most likely a popular person in school – a real people person.

All in all we have played a simple game that has neverthe-less afforded us a window on a wide range of human perception and behavior. If we are somewhat content with the utility of this model, then we can start to take this ball and run with it. This is only the beginning. This is the easy way to understand human perception, and it promises to give us much insight into the human condition.

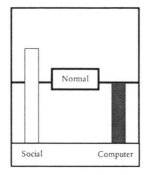

Figure 1.10 Personable perception

For example, we can see now why psychology has been so challenged in addressing the mind and perception. Psychology treats the act of human perception as one thing that comes in different forms. But, these pictures suggest that perception is made up of social and computer thinking, and that the level of each in relation to the other determines what kind of person each of us can become. *It's these two kinds of thinking, social and computer, that integrate to form our perception.*

Furthermore, we can also begin to understand why brain neuroscience is challenged when it comes to finding out how the brain supports perception. What is needed is an agenda for studying the way the brain creates social and computer thinking. What is needed is an exploration of the brain to discover the control system that maintains both kinds of thinking in relation to one another.

The fact is that current diagnosis of autism is something that is performed on a qualitative basis. That means the analyst has to use his or her own better judgement. There is sometimes a bit of confusion regarding the difference between high-functioning autism and Asperger's syndrome, for example. A trip to

see five different analysts may very well yield five different professional qualifications about any one client.

Real-life examples

Armed with our new understanding of perception as being
made up of social and computer thinking, we now have
afforded ourselves a new way of getting a handle on perception
and the behavior it supports. Let's take some real-life examples,
and see how they might be described with our simple pictures.

Leonardo da Vinci

He was probably way, way above normal on both the social and
the computer because he was able to move with ease through
the social and political worlds of his day and he is recognized
as being gifted mechanically and very design-oriented. He was
an all-round genius – a rare person indeed.

Bill Gates

He is able to dominate in the business world as well as demon-
strating computer brilliance and autistic behaviors such as lack
of eye contact and rocking back and forth a lot. He has all the
characteristics of a geek, but to me a geek is a person who is
high on the computer and somewhere around average on the
social – a person who is slightly autistic. But, Gates is more
than a geek because he is so adept at business management. He
has a unique ability to excel in business management as well as
computer science. There are not many people that can do both
so well. His business acumen suggests he is above average on
the social and his computer science brilliance indicates he is
way above average on the computer.

Bill Clinton

Almost the opposite of Bill Gates! Here is a person who is way, way above normal on the social, and perhaps above normal on the computer. His computer thinking was high enough to support his activity as a scholarship student, but his social thinking is so high as to make him one of the great public speakers of our time. His social presentation and public speaking skills go far beyond words. His commanding presence and impeccable composure are the giveaway of super-high social thinking.

Ghandi

Probably average on the social and way above average on the computer because he was always on the outside looking in, so to speak. He was a brilliant philosopher and attorney but tended to prefer living outside of normal social life. He had a gift for defying social convention. Everything about this man's life suggests he was not the least bit concerned with being normal. Nothing about him was normal, yet his vision was so sublime that he changed the normal world itself.

Albert Einstein

Probably average on the social and way, way above average on the computer because he spent the last decades of his life as a social recluse after giving the world some of the most brilliant mathematical models ever. By the way, one of Einstein's sons also became a physicist, but the other was institutionalized for schizophrenia. It is possible that schizophrenia itself might be characterized by a dramatic slide from normal social thinking to far below normal social thinking.

Ronald Reagan

Well, he was probably way above average on the social and average on the computer because he, much like George W. Bush, had an uncanny genius for social presentation. He was not known for having intellectual prowess, but it didn't matter. People liked him, and they liked to like him. He had a knack for social presentation that was disarming, warm, and congenial. Don't forget, he was a successful professional actor in Hollywood long before he entered politics – a real social genius.

By the way, former President Reagan had Alzheimer's disease in the last decade of his life, and it is also possible that Alzheimer's, like schizophrenia, produces a slide from normal social thinking to far below normal social thinking.

★ ★ ★

We have already accomplished so much. In this first chapter, with the help of a few simple pictures, we have allowed ourselves to engage an understanding of autism and human perception. And, this is only the beginning.

In the next chapter we will begin considering exactly what it means to have the computer thinking higher than the social thinking. Exactly what does it mean to say that a person has more difficulty doing normal social life than most people? What does it mean to be normal anyway? What is particularly fascinating to me about this approach is that the more we understand autism, the more we understand normalcy, and vice versa.

So, we will spend a little time considering exactly what normal people do that makes them normal. We will see a simple image of two kinds of thinking working together to give us our perception of the world. When we see how normal perception supports normal behavior, we will have an immediate insight into the issues particular to autistic perception and behavior.

The social thinking has its job to do, as does the computer thinking. Depending upon how much of each type of thinking you have, a particular perception is produced by your brain as a result. Your behavior can never go too far beyond the base it has in your brain's perception. *Social and computer thinking combine to form your perception. Your perception supports and enables your behavior.*

For present purposes, perception exists in terms of social and computer thinking, and how high one is in relation to the other. There are no neat and tidy boundary lines to be drawn. There are no boxes we can make up to pigeonhole people conveniently. When it comes to autistic perception we can already see that it is all shades of gray. Everyone has his or her own levels of social and computer thinking.

How would you draw a picture of yourself?

Chapter Two

The Six Functions of Perception
How Social and Computer Thinking Work Together

Now that we have an idea how this model works, let's take it one step further and examine how social thinking and computer thinking work together. When we say that social thinking is lower in autistic perception, the direct implication is that the functions of social thinking aren't shoring up an individual's perception as strongly as the computer thinking. When the function of computer thinking is doing most of the work, the result is perception that can be recognized as autistic. But it is not enough just to say that autistic perception is the result of less social thinking than computer thinking.

Autistic perception is something that can actually be recognized in terms of the chief characteristics of computer thinking itself. Also, autistic perception is more fully understood by learning the five functions of social thinking, the corresponding main function of computer thinking, and how they work together. Once we understand this we can begin imagining what it must be like to have far less of a disposition to experience the five functions of social thinking. We can imagine what it must be like to have one's perception governed chiefly by the main function of computer thinking.

The big picture

Social thinking and computer thinking work together to create our perception of the world. All of our perception and behavior is the result of our social thinking and our computer thinking working together. But how do we know what each one does and how they both work together?

A wealth of research in social psychology focuses on the cognitive thought processes underlying our behavior. This research indicates that several categories of thought are at work subjectively, or mentally, as we calculate behavior for each social situation we encounter. These categories of thought are actually grounded in the inductive work of social thinking. The calculation of the actual behavior itself is grounded in the deductive work of computer thinking.

Social thinking has five specific functions:

1.   defining the situation

2.   locating social identities

3.   seeing the world through the eyes of others

4.   supporting assumptions of normalcy

5.   gauging time and timing.

These functions work together to allow us to enter a situation and to answer the question "What is going on here?"

Computer thinking has one specific function: computing appropriate behavior. Computer thinking takes the answer to the question "What is going on here?" and uses that information to compute appropriate behavior for each situation.

This is the big picture. This is how social thinking and computer thinking work together to create perception. The social thinking decides what is going on in our surroundings. It scans the environment for meaningful information. Using that information, our computer thinking computes the best behavior for that situation. Initially, this takes place on a nonconscious level. That is, it is an automatic function of the brain. It is only with much practice and effort that we can become increasingly aware of our perception of the world. Taking responsibility for our perception is a big part of growing up. But, even in a highly developed and sophisticated human being, most of this activity is performed automatically on a nonconscious level.

Let's take a look at the five functions of social thinking and then we'll consider the main function of computer thinking.

Defining the social situation: The first function

Whether we realize it or not, every single time we enter into a social situation our brain has to calculate what the situation actually must be. The brain has to do this first in order to know what to do in that situation. Our brain's social thinking kicks in and delivers the news in a virtually automatic fashion. It does this so well that we usually don't even think about it much.

This is a heavyweight concept subscribed to by all sociologists. The fact that this act of cognition must take place inside every person's mind makes it one of the virtual starting points of social psychology. Think about it. If you could not define the social situation for one entire day, then you would not know where you are right now. If you did not know where you are right now, then you would not know how to behave right now. If you did not know where you are right now or how to behave right now, then you would certainly want some help finding your way back home.

But, what would happen if you could not define the social situation every single day of your life? Well, you would not know how to calculate behavior for social situations, and you might not even realize that you did not know. If you had absolutely no way of defining situations, then you probably would not be able to appear sane. And if I were somehow able to magically turn off your ability to define the social situation right now, you might be stuck in exactly the same place you are right now for an indefinite period of time. You would not necessarily know when it was time to move or change situations. Moreover, when you did have to enter a new social situation it could be disturbing and troublesome for you. It might even be downright traumatizing.

For example, you have to be able to know that you are entering the workplace in order to know how to act appropriately in the workplace. You have to know that you are entering home in order to know how to behave at home. It should be evident by now that the lower one's social thinking, the lower one's ability to define the social situation, and this will be a part of an autistic person's experience. In other words, the stronger the autistic perception, the more difficulty a person has defining the social situation.

This is one of the single greatest markers of our social thinking. Not only do we have an ability constantly to define our social situation, but we also have a highly developed ability to sense the emotions that are appropriate for our social situation. Without this important function of social thinking, we could not perform the rites of social pride and social humiliation that are so important to the normal world. In many ways, the amount of pride you can gather for yourself and the amount of humiliation you can forestall are directly related to how well you can define social situations.

People with autistic perception have difficulty understanding the drama of pride and humiliation that unfolds in social life. People with high-functioning autism or Asperger's syndrome will often have enough social thinking to desire making friends and having a social life. At the same time, normal people might recognize them as odd before too much time has passed. At that point the autistic person becomes a ripe candidate for social humiliation. This can take many forms. But what can be peculiar sometimes is that the autistic person may not be quite as aware of, or quite as bothered by, the humiliation. To them it may just be the price of admission to the social world. It might not even be all that disturbing to them.

At the same time, a person who is above normal on social thinking and slightly higher still on computer thinking may have yet a different experience. This person may never be labeled as, say, Asperger's syndrome, but in terms of the way we are looking at social thinking and computer thinking we have to recognize them as slightly autistic. They may just be perceived as weird, odd, and a geek, book smart with no common sense.

Whereas a person with lower social thinking might endure social humiliation happily, this person who is hard to qualify and label, but still slightly autistic, might have a different response. They might become eccentric and full of pride. Repetitive behaviors might take the form of an obsession with one topic of interest. They might join MENSA (an organization for bright people) or go to graduate school. They might even hold the normal world in contempt. This is because their high computer thinking places them on the outside looking in on social life. Such people will never qualify as normal, yet they know they are brilliant and above average in intelligence.

Locating social identities: The second function

It is a part of our social learning – we have to be able to know what identity to locate for others and ourselves in each social situation. We also have to know that the identities in one situation may very well change roles in another situation. Sociologists emphasize the importance of being able to situate identities relative to their social surroundings. The very act of recognizing someone's social identity in a particular time and space is one of the most important concepts in social psychology.

This part of our social thinking allows us to conceive of having a significant other. As our social thinking generalizes its knowledge and experience we are able eventually to conceive of a generalized other. This is the level of social awareness that allows us to conceptualize of a public or a society at large. It's what allows us to use the universal "they" as in "they say coffee is bad for you," or "what will they think of next?"

Let's suppose you work with your spouse. You have to be able to locate the identity of your spouse at home and again at work. In each social situation you have to be able to assign a different role to the same identity. You can't act the same way with your spouse at work as you do at home. Home is a private place and work is a public place. And you have to be able to locate the social identity of your spouse at home or in the workplace in order to know how to behave appropriately in each social situation.

It takes years for children to learn how to do these things in a way that passes as normal. Lots of laughter and lots of tears will pass as a child learns to negotiate the difference between public situations and private situations, between "mom at home" and "mom in the grocery store," for instance. Children will engage imaginative play for years in which they rehearse various social situations, the identities, and the roles that go along with them. But the stronger the autistic perception, the less likely a child will be doing these things.

Sometimes people with autism like to make up nicknames for people. This is an example of creative social thinking. It shows that people with autism are actually capable of locating social identities and can even enjoy being creative about it. I think normal people are so stuck on trying to understand autism in terms of normalcy that they lose the opportunity to consider how autistic perception might be varied and diverse. Social thinking exists in autistic perception. But we have to become accustomed to the notion that there are many variations of social thinking that must exist outside of normal perception.

People with autism register the world around them. They may not perceive it in the same terms as a normal person, but they register information about the environment. Sometimes they register more information than a normal person would. They may simply have their own ways of registering social identities.

For children to learn to define social situations and then properly locate identities with their proper roles requires lots of practice. But they can only do it in the first place if their brain is wired with enough social thinking to support the activity.

Seeing the world through the eyes of others: The third function

We have to see the world through other people's eyes in order to engage the fullest extent of interactive experience. This is so critically important, not just so we can empathize with others, but actually for what it means to our own sense of self. In psychology they call it perspective taking, and in sociology they call it role taking. Indeed, this ability to see yourself through another person's eyes is the mental activity required to achieve a full-blown sense of self. This concept is from a special branch of social psychology called symbolic interactionism. Here is how it works.

Imagine you are two and a half years old. It is time to eat. Your mother serves the food. Tonight you are having rice. But, as soon as you see the rice, you decide to have some fun. You pick up some rice and throw it across the room. But your mother does not think this is very funny. In fact, she gets angry and scolds you. It seems that throwing rice is an action that causes grief for your mother, and, consequently, for you too.

Now, let's move into the future a few days. Tonight mother is serving rice again. And sure enough, as soon as it is served it occurs to you that it would be fun to throw some rice across the room. But then you remember the previous time you threw the rice. You remember this made your mother angry. You relive the moment in which you threw the rice, and how your mother let you know that you were being bad. You reason that if you do not throw the rice your mother will see you as good. And you are now able to conclude this line of reasoning in the following way. "Tonight I am not throwing rice and my mom sees me as being good. This is how mom sees me, and this is how I see myself."

In that moment a sense of self is born. It is precisely this ability to see yourself the way others see you that is so important to attaining a sense of self. It is precisely this ability to become a social object to yourself, the same way you appear as a social object to others, that helps you to objectify a sense of your own self.

When you can see yourself as a social object the same way you appear as a social object to others, then you are on your way to achieving a self-concept. In fact, it is this ability to see yourself through the eyes of others that is directly related to the ability to recognize your own reflection in a mirror.

People with strong autistic perception can't recognize their own reflection in a mirror. The reason is that they have less social thinking and can't support the activity of seeing themselves through the eyes of others in the first place. So, they can't take the role of the mirror image and realize it is themselves looking at themselves. The ability to reflect back onto yourself mentally is critical to social life.

Autistic people will sometimes refer to themselves in the third person. This is because they have less of an ability to see themselves through the eyes of others, and resolve that experience as a self-concept. Instead of saying, "I have to go now," I might say, "Alex has to go now." This is lower social thinking unable to achieve this full-blown sense of self. The autistic child has a sense of self. But the autistic child is not able to engage the same perspective on itself as a normal person. Instead, the autistic person treats himself or herself exactly the same way others treat them.

This is also the reason autistic children tend not to engage in imaginary play as other children do. Imaginary play is entirely based on the ability to see oneself through the eyes of another. Imaginary play requires the ability to adopt the perspective of another being. This is difficult for an autistic child to do. An autistic child lives in more of a literal, two-dimensional world. Other children will play house. The autistic child will line up his cars exactly the same way over and over again.

This ability to see yourself through the eyes of another is a high-level cognitive abstraction of everyday reality. Once again, it is one of the hallmarks of our social thinking. For example, one has to be able to see oneself through the eyes of others in order to become aware of fashion trends and the importance of following them. If you could not see yourself as others see you, it would be virtually impossible for you to become a slave to fashion, let alone hold a meaningful conversation with anyone.

Of course, none of us are very good at this. We are always second-guessing others and ourselves wondering what the other person meant to say, and misinterpreting what they really did say. That is why any of us can end up in counseling and therapy sessions. But the less social thinking people have wired into their brain, the less they will be able to gauge how other people see them, and the less they will even care in the first place.

It is a myth perpetuated by professionals that autism is a state of mind with no self. The experience of self varies with the level of social thinking. Autistic people have self, they just have trouble expressing themselves appropriately. They don't have the same view of themselves that normal people do. For a person with strong autistic perception, self may be experienced in abstract and mystical ways that are detached from the more concrete everyday experience of self shared by normal people.

The functions of social thinking not only compute what is going on in social situations, but they ground us emotionally in social life so that we actually find ourselves caring about what other people think. We end up caring how we look to others, and constantly monitoring the environment for evidence that we are doing a good job of impressing others with our mastery of normal behavior. But without full-blown social thinking you don't monitor the social environment as effectively, and you don't even care.

When you see someone who wears his or her hair the same way for 20 years you really have to wonder about his or her level of social thinking. When you see someone who wears clothes that are completely out of style, or who wears the same clothes over and over again, it ought to make you wonder. However, it doesn't have to make you wonder what is wrong with that person. That would be the normal response.

Whenever I see someone like that, it makes me wonder if I haven't stumbled across someone whose computer thinking might be considerably higher than their social thinking.

At that point, knowing what I know, I feel almost excited and immediately sympathetic. I think, "This person must be slightly autistic." I start to wonder what life is like for them. I wonder how I might communicate to them that I understand them a little better than most people. I also know that this person probably will not care too much about whether or not I am sympathetic, so I don't want to offend them by gushing all over them.

One of the most important keys to communicating with people who are high on computer thinking, and relatively lower on social thinking, is to reflect their behavior, especially their repetitive behaviors. If you can find a way to reflect their perception or behavior back to them, then they will have an experience of sympathetic communication. They may not like you, but they may appreciate you. It is to be hoped that people will understand more and more exactly why they might look for ways to reflect autistic perception and behavior in order to communicate better with autistic people. It is difficult for an autistic person to see the world through your eyes. But it is easy for them to register that their repetitive behavior is being reflected. It is better for you to do that and help them to achieve identification with another in interaction than to wait for them to see the world through your eyes.

Invoking the assumptions of normalcy: The fourth function

The assumptions of normalcy represent a strange code that is omnipresent in normal social life. The field of sociolinguistics tells us that these assumptions of normalcy are the very glue of social life. The assumptions of normalcy must be invoked and used continually in order for social interaction to take place. It is the assumptions of normalcy that allow us to assume social interaction will be meaningful and successful. We absolutely must be able to invoke these assumptions in order to be able to participate in normal social life. At the same time, the stronger one's autistic perception, the less one will be invoking these assumptions because they are a function of social thinking.

There are essentially four assumptions of normalcy:

1. "When I communicate with other people, they will understand me."

2. "When other people communicate with me, I will understand them."

3. "If I don't understand other people now, I'll figure out what they meant later."

4. "If I don't figure it out later, then it doesn't really matter anyway."

The fact is that you would need help navigating the social world unless you were able to invoke these assumptions of normalcy. You would be like a stranger in a strange land if you had to question everything that took place in every conversation. Without the assumptions of normalcy how would one even begin to implicate oneself in ongoing social life?

So often when someone gives us directions we are not very sure how we will be able to follow them. But we always act as if we do, and we proceed on the faith that we will get there somehow, even if we have to ask for more directions along the way! We do this by invoking the assumptions of normalcy.

These are explicitly social assumptions using social thinking. They must be invoked as an axiomatic, or baseline, assumption, and all social interaction proceeds on the basis of these assumptions. They allow us to generalize about the nature of our meaningful experience. Because we can invoke assumptions of normalcy we are able smoothly to perpetuate our meaningful experience from one moment to the next without full conscious knowledge of every detail in our perception. This would be too much for us to compute as we move through day-to-day events.

Social life would come to a grinding halt if people had to confirm full understanding of every single thing that was said to them. The assumptions of normalcy allow us to take our meaningful experience for granted, instead of questioning everything that happens as we move seamlessly from one moment to the next.

Conversely, in strong autistic perception we have an experience that is much more literal. This perception relies on "If-Then" sequences of action. So, if this person is in a new situation it will not be possible to assume normalcy and to take for granted that all is well. This person will not be able to know with assuredness that a mutual understanding can be achieved.

Marriages fail and relationships fall asunder when the assumptions of normalcy no longer function in their natural capacities. When the assumptions of normalcy are not at work in social interaction it becomes increasingly difficult to maintain focus and commitment to any one version of reality.

In fact, a recipe for driving someone else crazy is simply to suspend the assumptions of normalcy in interaction. There was a sociological experiment in which college students were instructed to return home for Thanksgiving break and question every aspect of their parents' speech. For example, if parents ask "How do you like school?" the students were instructed to respond with something like "What do you mean by like, do you mean appreciate or enjoy?" To which the parent might respond "Well, how do you enjoy your classes?" To which the student might respond "Well, do you really want to know about every single class, or just the teachers I like?" How long can this go on before parents question their children's sanity? Not long at all. Students reported how difficult it was to suspend these assumed understandings that underlie every conversation.

Try it sometime. Try going against the grain and doing something that is not expected of you. Try doing something that is never done in social life. It is rather difficult to do. All of this demonstrates the tenuous and complex achievement of social thinking every day all day long. It further clarifies what is not happening as much in strong autistic perception. There are numerous assumptions of meaning and understanding that must be mutually upheld by all parties concerned in every interaction all day long. The stronger the autistic perception the less the individual will be able to skate on the thin ice of these assumptions of normalcy.

If you had to carry a grammar book and a dictionary with you everywhere you went in order to make precisely sure that what you are saying is correct and intelligible, then normal conversation would come to a screeching halt. Normal conversation proceeds much more on the basis of assumptions of normalcy than anything else. And if conversation ever becomes meaningless it might be because the assumptions of normalcy have been halted or violated.

For example, attorneys are expert manipulators of the assumptions of normalcy. In a trial, when an attorney questions the meaning of every phrase, term, and nuance that is being used, sooner or later all sense of normalcy vanishes. At this point reasonable doubt becomes the order of the day. All you have to do, if you want to shut down a conversation, is begin to question every single statement that is being made. Are you sure about that? Why? Really? I'm not sure about that. What do you mean by this word? Exactly how would you define that word? Search for too much clarity and the conversation ends in the dark.

In a friendly conversation we constantly communicate agreement and the assumption that we understand the other person, that we know what the other person means. If you are constantly unsure about the other person's meaning, then the other person becomes uneasy. By now it should be apparent that social thinking is always greasing the wheels of social interaction.

It's not so much that we know exactly what is going on in the situation and in other people's minds, it's just that we care enough to keep assuming that we will get clarity later if we continue assuming normalcy at the moment. Social life is an orchestration of mutually assumed realities.

Gauging time and timing: The fifth function

The fifth and final function of social thinking revolves around the ability to gauge time and timing. To have a sense of timing is critically important in social life. The above four functions we have just addressed are based in an ability to know what time it is. It is a part of locating ourselves accurately as we move through the three-dimensional world. As soon as we move through space, we move through time. And this three- and four-dimensional thinking is what social thinking is all about.

The perception of time in autism is of particular interest. Our experience of time is grounded in our social thinking. Our ability to gauge time and timing is intimately related to the functions of social thinking. We use social thinking to navigate the world in a meaningful way. One of the critical hallmarks in a child's cognitive development is the ability to tell time. We expect normal people to know what time it is. We all take for granted our ability to be on time and to have a sense of timing that aligns us with the normal world.

But a person with severe autism is not able to generalize from one situation to the next. Their world is much more two-dimensional than that of a normal person. The very experience of time itself is a mystery to a person with very strong autistic perception. Often people with strong autism will be fascinated by watches and clocks. Since social thinking implies the ability to define social situations and navigate our transition from one situation to another, a person with much lower social thinking will not be able to move from one moment to the next in a fluid way.

The passage of time itself is a mystery of perpetual movement that challenges the person with strong computer thinking. Computer thinking stays the same, and does the same thing over and over again. But the ticking of a clock, and the passage of time itself, defies this perception. On the one hand, it is rhythmic and precise. On the other hand, it is always changing and reinventing itself as it progresses from one moment to the next. In this way, the passage of time itself is a great mystery for a person with strong autistic perception. Everything about change is challenging for a person who has higher computer thinking than social thinking. Anything that requires change is difficult for an autistic person.

Computing behavior: The sixth function

If social thinking tells us the "Who, What, Where, When, and Why" of social interaction, then computer thinking tells us "How" to behave accordingly. The logic of computer thinking is deductive logic. That means specific information is automatically computed to reveal specific results. On the basis of information provided by the five functions of social thinking, our computer thinking has one main function: to compute appropriate behavior.

Computer thinking always does the same thing in the same way. It is repetitive, machine-like, and completely consistent. Since this is the logic that computes our behavior, it is obvious how important this is to the world. We must always be able to depend on consistent calculation of proper behavior. It is the dependability of our computer thinking that allows us to create and uphold manners and rules for etiquette. The very idea of normal behavior is grounded in our ability always to calculate proper behavior in the same way. We depend on our computer thinking to make our behavior consistent.

When we stand in an elevator, our computer thinking always calculates the same behaviors for each of us. The elevator is a good place to see the power of our computer thinking. Its function is to calculate behavior and its characteristic is to do so in a repetitive and predictable way. Nowhere is this as evident as in a typical elevator ride. We enter an elevator. Our social thinking kicks in and defines the situation, locates the identities and roles, sees itself through everyone else's eyes, invokes assumptions of normalcy, and gauges time and timing.

Then our computer thinking takes this information and calculates the appropriate behavior. And this behavior is always the same! We look at our shoes, we look at the numbers over the door with seeming interest, we look at our watch – and we would never dare do much else. This is the power of computer thinking. It calculates with great precision and pre-dictability, always giving the same results.

It seems that people with enough social thinking to engage the functions of social thinking fully do so in a more or less automatic way. Just through experience in social life we soak up the ability to do these things well enough to pass as normal. But if they don't come naturally, the first problem is that the person themselves will not even realize it. The second problem is that they will be challenged by the daunting task of having to force themselves to learn.

Often, people with less social thinking than computer thinking will just opt out. That is, they will prefer to be alone. Over time they will forgo the routines of normal social life in favor of a life that does not require full use of the functions of social thinking. This may be interpreted as an intelligent strategy, a survival function invoked by someone who has less social thinking wired into their brain and who has more trouble invoking the functions of social thinking.

In cases of strong autistic perception there is more difficulty than mere awkwardness with social functions. The functions of social thinking are used to answer the question "What is going on here?" If a person does not have enough social thinking to compute the answer, they will not have enough information to feed into their computer thinking. Our computer thinking computes appropriate behavior based entirely on the information provided by our social thinking.

In other words, a person with higher computer thinking and relatively low social thinking will not always have enough information to compute proper behavior. At that point they are steeped in computer thinking, which is continually overshadowing their lower social thinking.

If a person is unable to compute social behavior and they are left in a world of pure computer thinking, oblivious to their social surroundings, that person is strongly autistic. That person's behavior will not be grounded in social life. That person's behavior will be grounded in their own strong experience of computer thinking.

Beginning to understand autism

Our challenge is not so much with the autistic perception and behavior itself. The real problem lies within our own rigid confines of normalcy. Autistic people exhibit rigid, obsessive behavior patterns. But normal people are just as rigid and obsessive about being normal! A major theme of this book is that we are all autistic to one extent or another because we all have computer thinking built into our perception. Sociologically speaking, there is a cult of normalcy that is just as rigid and obsessive about its behavior patterns as any autistic person.

The less social thinking a person has, and the more autistic their perception is, the more difficulty they will have with all of these functions of social thinking. In order to present oneself as normal to others a person has to be able continually to define the social situation, locate identities and their proper roles in those situations, see oneself as a social object through the eyes of others, and invoke the assumptions of normalcy. If a person has difficulty doing these things, they will have difficulty when it comes to learning to do them or even learning to fake them.

We now have a big picture of human perception that is made up of social and computer thinking. If a person's computer thinking is higher than their social thinking they will be engaging some kind of autistic perception. The stronger the autistic perception the more difficulty that person will have invoking the functions of social thinking.

Social thinking infers what is going on around us in every social situation, and computer thinking computes the behavior that is appropriate to each social situation. But if a person can't adequately infer what is going on in the social situation, then they will not have enough information to compute appropriate behavior. At that point, the person will be noticeably different. They will not qualify for the hallowed world of normalcy, and others will scrutinize their behavior.

Furthermore, such a person who has considerably less social thinking would have less of a normal perspective on themselves and less emotional commitment to social life. They would be magnetically drawn into a world of pure computer thinking. With less social information, the computer thinking is less able to compute appropriate behavior, and left more and more to its own devices. Such a person will seem to be in his or her own world, and indeed they are. But, that does not mean they are not having their own meaningful experience!

A few examples

Let's take one social situation and see how different levels of social thinking might handle that situation. Let's consider a ten-year-old boy or girl making a trip to a new local mall with their family for the very first time.

A person with social thinking that is far below normal and computer thinking that is normal (probably labeled autistic, see Figure 1.2) would have an enormous amount of difficulty, especially if it was the first time. Their family would not look forward to taking them because they don't conform easily to normal social situations. Since the social is so low, first-time social situations can be traumatic for autistic people. This person would be flooded with data from all sides, none of it making any sense. It would be a difficult experience emotionally for the person and for whoever accompanied them to the mall. It is possible that with a little practice this person might be able to develop a routine for making this trip, and we will discuss this later in the book. But with little ability to define the social situation, locate all the social identities, see themselves through the eyes of others, invoke assumptions of normalcy, and gauge time and timing, this person might not have a very good time.

A person with social thinking that is below normal and computer thinking that is normal (probably labeled high-functioning autistic, see Figure 1.3) would be able to enjoy the experience, but their enjoyment would take peculiar forms. For example, they might tend to become focused on a piece of gum stuck to the floor. They would stoop to examine it. Their family would continue walking until suddenly noticing that this person is not with them. Upon finding the person and asking them to come along, this person might remain oblivious. The family might resort to begging and demanding that the person come along. But this person could be completely entranced by the fact that the entire floor is clean with the exception of this piece of gum. Other family members might want to shop or visit with friends, but there is a good chance that they will end up cleaning this gum off the floor before resuming their normal agenda. This person could talk about the gum for the rest of the day – this was a fun experience for them.

A person with normal social thinking and considerably above normal computer thinking (they might be labeled Asperger's syndrome or they might not be labeled at all, see Figure 1.4) would be able to enjoy the experience because they are essentially normal in terms of social thinking. But their higher computer thinking would exert a magnetic pull away from the social. Look for them to end up in the bookstore, content to read books for hours.

Their family would do well to leave them there, agreeing to meet back at the bookstore in an hour to check on them. They probably won't wander off because they would have little or no desire to shop for clothes, study the latest fashions, or socialize. They would probably be a lot happier engaging some repetitive obsessive behavior like reading history books, or maybe playing arcade games. If they were forced to shop for clothes, they would probably buy something that is exactly like what they already have at home in their closet, preferring to wear the same style over and over again.

Now, let's reverse the scenarios in terms of the social and the computer.

A person with normal social thinking and computer thinking that is far below normal (probably labeled as having "severe learning difficulties," see Figure 1.8) would probably be happy to spend time with their family anywhere, especially if they got some ice cream somewhere along the way. But, their family would not look forward to taking them because their computer thinking is so low they can't compute appropriate behavior, and this becomes risky out in public.

A person with social thinking that is normal and computer thinking that is below normal (probably labeled as having "moderate learning difficulties," or Down's syndrome, see Figure 1.9) would be able to enjoy the trip thoroughly. This would be a fun-filled trip because it is all about social excitement. This person would crave social life and social interaction, and they would be able to have a lot of fun.

A person with social thinking considerably above normal and normal computer thinking (probably a popular person at school, see Figure 1.10) would really be in their element. What could be better than studying the latest fashions, buying clothes, getting a cool haircut, checking out the latest music, and socializing with friends who are there also?

A different kind of perception

By playing around with the levels of social and computer thinking we can address a wide range of human experience. We can see that higher computer thinking leads to autistic perception and behaviors. These tend to run outside of normal social life. We can see that higher social thinking leads to very sociable and interactive personalities who are thrilled by the trappings of the normal world. We can see that having exceedingly low social or computer thinking would present challenges to families in terms of the actual safety of the person concerned.

With this model of social and computer thinking working together to describe a person's perception we are now prepared to go further into the world of autistic perception.

We say people "suffer" from autism. Autism is not specifically a state of suffering. *In fact, autistic perception is a different kind of meaningful perception.* Autism has its own rewards. The single greatest problem with autism is that normal people don't understand it. If normal people could learn to accept autistic perception as a different kind of meaningful perception, then people who work with people who have autism could begin to relax a little bit. In other words, teachers and counselors working with autistic people have a tremendous burden to carry because the normal world automatically labels autism in its own normal terms. But, if we begin to understand autism, then maybe we can begin to value autistic people on their own terms instead of devaluing them on ours.

Autism challenges our assumptions of normalcy more starkly than most kinds of perception and behavior. Not only do autistic people tend to look normal, they often are beautiful. Not only do they tend to be intelligent, they tend to exhibit unusual heights of intelligence. For these reasons, normal people and scientists are absolutely confounded by autism. Imagine beholding a child who is strikingly beautiful in his or her physical appearance, exhibits precocious intellectual abilities in certain areas, and seems rather indifferent to the most basic social graces. Since psychology tends to label a person as either normal or not normal, autistic people challenge those tightly defined categories in a way that leaves most of us unsettled.

Exactly what it means to be in a world of pure computer thinking will be the topic of the next chapter. We will begin to analyze the nature of that experience in ways that will help us to understand and communicate with people in that state. We are beginning to understand autism.

Chapter Three

Exploring the Experience of Autism

We have addressed the way social and computer thinking make up our perception. We have taken a look at the functions of social and computer thinking and the way they work together. At this point we are ready to begin taking careful stock of the nature of autistic perception.

Social thinking reflects the concept of inductive logic. Computer thinking reflects the concept of deductive logic. For the sake of understanding autism let's assume that computer thinking is basically the same as deductive logic. What I am suggesting here is that the characteristics of deductive logic are the characteristics of autistic perception.

A perfect example of the deductive logic in computer thinking is 2 + 2 = 4. If I give you two apples, and if I give you two more apples, then I have given you four apples. It is unthinkable that anyone could argue with this conclusion. It is always the same regardless of the social situation. How could it be any other way? This is the very logic of computers, robots, and electronics. You can set your clock by this logic and you can count your money using this logic. It's that important and it's that powerful.

Computer thinking has some very definite characteristics. It takes specific information and gives specific results. It gives automatic, guaranteed, predictable results. It's always the same, and attempting to change or challenge the way it works is almost like violating a law of nature.

What is it like to be autistic?

One good way to describe computer thinking is that it works in terms of rules for action. Computer thinking can be described as the kind of thinking that makes statements that always say "If…, then…": "If I give you 2 + 2, then I give you 4." If you flip the switch, then the light turns off. If you flip the switch again, then the light turns on again. If this, then that. If this, then that. If this, then that. Everything is always If-Then.

The strong experience of If-Then thinking explains why people with strong autistic perception often enjoy collecting things. If they have very strong autistic perception, they might insist on keeping a set of objects arranged in a specific way. As we move into ranges of high-functioning autism and high levels of slight autism, we will find a predilection for collecting things, but not normal things! For example, we will see a person fussing over their collection, but we may have no idea what they are collecting. I once heard of an autistic girl who collected things she had found in alleys. Her thinking was: "If I find it in an alley, then I can put it in my collection."

The collections will be a reflection of something that is meaningful to them. They will decide what to collect, and it will probably not be a normal collection. By the way, this is also an excellent example of the creative thinking that lies inside computer thinking. When an autistic person makes up his or her own unique collection, it is an example of creative computer thinking.

So, the love of collections reflects If-Then computer thinking. If I collect matchbooks, and I see a matchbook, then I can put it in my collection. At high levels of slight autism, the tendency to collect may take the form of an obsession with a certain topic of knowledge or inquiry. This person is effectively collecting pieces of knowledge, and they will attain expertise in their chosen area of interest.

Now, if you can imagine that this is the way autistic people think, then you have a huge insight into the way that their mind works. Let's consider a person with very strong autistic perception. For example, somebody whose social thinking is far below their computer thinking. We are talking about a person who most people would easily agree is autistic.

Once we have a good insight into this person, we will only have to loosen the parameters to envision the whole range of autistic perception. Once we know this person, we will have a great insight into even slightly autistic perception and behavior. The trick here is to consider the social and the computer together.

When we are talking about a person who has very, very low social thinking and normal computer thinking, we have to combine the characteristics of computer thinking with the notion that there is little activity supporting the functions of social thinking.

This gives us a person anchored in repetitive, automatic, predictable thinking, while at the same time relatively free from the norms of defining social situations. This gives us a person who will be considerably challenged when it comes to defining situations, locating identities in social situations, seeing themselves through the eyes of others, calling on the assumptions of normalcy, and gauging time and timing.

What would it be like to walk into a social situation and to be free from the experience of defining that situation? What if it just didn't happen in your mind? What if you had no real concern with locating identities or imagining how people must be seeing you through their eyes? What if you didn't particularly care about the normal world?

You would be in a state of incredible freedom! To others you would seem to be out of it. But you wouldn't even be thinking about others in the first place. You would be experiencing a tremendous amount of freedom. So much freedom, in fact, that it might be difficult to handle at times.

At the same time, in order to frame your meaningful experience you might develop very rigid patterns of behavior in relation to the passage of time. Since you can't generalize over time and space, you only think in terms of If-Then, If-Then. So you might develop rituals of behavior that are fixated on time. If it is 7:00am, then it is time to get out of bed. If it is 7:05, then it is time to get dressed. You might be so fixed in your If-Then world of computer thinking that any deviation in your routines would come as a jarring shock to your system.

Now we are developing a sense of a person who experiences a tremendous amount of freedom. Yet in an effort to ground themselves in a meaningful experience of reality, they will become fixed in routines of action. This person has a meaningful experience of the world. It is just not fully grounded in the social world. It will be grounded in a reality that is based in repetitive routines of behavior. This person will be very rigid in their social behavior while their perception will be very free of social constraints.

Once I saw Donna Williams on television being interviewed and I remember her saying that when she was little and she went into the yard, she was not standing in the grass, she was standing in a riot of green. Think about this. The simple act of standing in the yard becomes a surreal experience.

This implies that the functions of social thinking also serve as filters that screen out all but the most normal meaningful experience. In some sense, we are all standing in a riot of green when we are standing on the grass. Yet, our social thinking filters out the barrage of incoming data and focuses on the most appropriate way to condense our sensory experience.

The act of having a normal meaningful perception of the world is the sophisticated accomplishment of a brain wired up to perform the functions of social thinking in an automatic way. The act of having an autistic meaningful perception is much more of a free-floating experience.

Whereas the sheer free-floating experience is not necessarily meaningful, where is meaning to be found for an autistic person? The answer lies in the notion that computer thinking automatically computes behavior based on the results of social thinking. If there is comparatively less social thinking, then the computer thinking kicks in, but it is left to its own devices. Since it is repetitive and automatic, we can expect it to begin computing repetitive behaviors automatically.

At this point the autistic person begins engaging some kind of repetitive, persevering behavior and indulging the mind with this behavior in an obsessive fashion. It is extremely important to recognize this as the meaningful behavior of a meaningful autistic perception of the world. It may not be meaningful to you, but it sure is meaningful to the autistic person. It is not necessarily easy to try forcing an autistic person to stop cold in the middle of repetitive, persevering behavior.

The fact that no one has been able to explain repetitive, persevering behavior in autism, and the fact that no one has a meaningful understanding of autism, are actually two sides of the same coin. However, our failure to miss the essence of autistic perception and behavior as an experience that is meaningful has only led to a succession of misunderstandings regarding autism.

For example, since the third function of social thinking, seeing yourself through the eyes of others, is the seat of self, so to speak, autistic perception will tend to be more selfless and transcendent. This is an abstract concept for most people, but it simply means that self is a very social thing to have, even though common sense tells us that it is a very private thing. Having a sense of self is a very social thing. Self is something we present to others. Self is interactive. But, when we lessen the social thinking, we lessen the interactive and reflective mental activities, and we also become freer from a normal sense of self.

Earlier I mentioned that autism used to be described as a state of mind with no self. But, to whatever extent there is social thinking, there will be some sense of self. However, since social thinking is so low in a person with strong autism, this person will have transcended the normal constraints of self, and will be experiencing something more like a state of uninhibited mental sequencing. People with autism have an experience of self, but a person with strong autism will experience self as a wisp of a cloud floating past the top of the Mount Everest of their mind. Most of the time it's just not going to be that important.

On the other hand, problems and challenges arise when people with autism are placed in first-time social situations. Exactly because they have a lesser ability to define the social situation, we ought to find ways to help them in and out of these first-time experiences.

Becoming autism-friendly: Making a social rehearsal video

One of the benefits of understanding autism is that we can become autism-friendly as a society. Businesses and professionals can let their communities and clients know that they are autism-friendly. This simply means that they are willing to accommodate autistic people and their families. These accommodations would arise from our understanding of autism. As one example of an autism-friendly activity let's consider a social rehearsal video that would allow autistic people to become familiar with an establishment before their first visit.

When autistic children need medical attention, for example, it can be difficult for all concerned. Especially when a person with autism is visiting for the first time. Health professionals could actually handle these situations in an autism-friendly manner. Part of understanding what it means to be autistic implies we can devise ways to help them communicate and interact with us. One of these ways may be to make a social rehearsal video for clients with autism on their first-time visit. The more severe the autism, the more difficulty will arise in the initial visit. A physician, a dentist, and any other practicing medical professional can make such a video and offer it to families who will be visiting their office.

The video should be about a typical visit to the office. It should begin out in the parking facility and continue on through a patient's typical visit to the office. It is especially important to include as many details as possible, no matter how seemingly insignificant they may be. This is a video that can be shown to the autistic child many, many times before making an actual visit. It might be a good idea to include some kind of reward at the beginning of the trip. For example, show some piece of candy or some little toy that will be offered at the beginning of the visit. Often children with autism enjoy fidgeting with something. Perhaps to give them a ball they can squeeze again and again is a nice gift. This might help to keep them distracted from the anxiety of a first-time visit, or from the general displeasure of having to wait in a line.

People with autism tend to have trouble waiting in lines, so the video should actually include a realistic waiting time before going in for the consultation. The person holding the camera should actually simulate each and every part of the actual visit. Walking in the door, interacting with service people behind the front desk, waiting in the waiting area, and an actual visit to the room where the consultation will take place.

The people in the video should speak to the camera as they would a live client. At the same time, the people in the office do not need to spend much time on the social graces themselves. A person with autism would prefer not to have strangers make eye contact, force a greeting, or touch them. People in the office should refer to the autistic person in the third person.

All of this might seem strange to a normal person. People in the normal world will tend to take a charitable perspective on the autistic person and go out of their way to try and be nice. This is the automatic response from normal people who have decided to be autism-friendly. But an understanding of autism reveals that social graces are not necessary or even desired! The less you pay attention to the autistic person, the more they will appreciate it. You make friends with an autistic person by not trying to make friends with them!

But you don't have to be high-tech to be autism-friendly either. Simply saying that you are autism-friendly is an act of communication with families of autism in and of itself. It is a way of extending trust, respect, safety, and comfort. Being autism-friendly is the fullest extent of the benefit that can be derived from this approach to understanding autism. It's the combination of our commitment to understanding the logic of our perception and our commitment to trust, respect, safety, and comfort that leads us to this concept of being autism-friendly. When you bring a full understanding of these concepts together the end result is an autism-friendly society.

Emotions and mental health

Imagine having emotions, but having little commitment to normal social life. Imagine not caring what is going on, what other people are doing, or what they are thinking about you. Imagine not caring if any effective communication ever takes place. Imagine having more important things to do! With the filters of social thinking dramatically dropped, the autistic person is emotionally committed to their repetitive, persevering behavior. This is what they care about the most.

Furthermore, in this state of mind, the normal world can become a scary place. What a horror to be forced to navigate one's way through this maze of social activity without having strong assumptions of normalcy to buffer you through your social day in a meaningful way. The worst thing that happens to an autistic person is having a normal person get in their face – especially someone who is trying to prevent them from continuing their repetitive behavior.

In a very real sense, the experience of repetitive, persevering behavior is probably the closest thing to an experience of mental health for an autistic person. This statement might seem to run counter to most people's expectations. But, what would be closer to mental health for an autistic person? Group therapy? Acting normal just to please others? No. Instead, since the nature of their mind is grounded in the deductive perception of computer thinking, the greatest sense of creature comfort they can experience will be derived from some activity that can be characterized as highly deductive. For example, it will be very mechanical, or design-oriented, or mathematical, or logical, or repetitive.

Mental health is all about experiencing trust, respect, safety, and comfort. Given the conditions that give rise to autistic perception, we must ask ourselves how we can make sure that autistic people have these things. Since an autistic person is so fragile in the face of social constraints and commitments, we must conclude that their experience of repetitive, persevering behaviors is their own version of a meaningful experience, and that it is an experience of mental health as well.

Of course, the concept of mental health as we know it is anchored in our concepts of normalcy. It is counter-intuitive, the last thing we would expect, to speak of autistic people having good mental health. But if we hold on to this model we have of social and computer thinking, we can begin to think of all human beings having the social and the computer thinking wired into their brain.

At this point it is interesting to consider the option of according every human the full dignity of their human experience regardless of where they fall on the continuum of perception. In other words, maybe we should rethink the way we define mental health. If mental health is a state of being that upholds the experience of trust, respect, safety, and comfort, then maybe a person who is fated to have perception that is not normal can nevertheless have their own experience of meaning and their own experience of mental health.

A person with autism does not perceive the world in a normal way, but they do register vast amounts of information. They have their own meaningful experience of the world through their own kind of perception that is anchored in computer thinking. Imagine what kind of loyalty an autistic person can display. For them a supportive relationship with someone who understands them will also become the emotional object of a repetitive, persevering commitment. Imagine what kind of selfless love they can hold in their hearts. Imagine how much trouble they would have expressing it to someone else.

Since autistic people have their own perception and emotions these emotions will be constrained along a much narrower line of experience – one that is characterized by repetitive behavior. They will get emotional, and they can be frustrated just like anyone else. They might even have more trouble getting over their frustration. Like an amplified feedback loop, this person might experience more frustration and more trouble getting over it, than anybody else realizes. They will also tend to have much more difficulty expressing their emotions in a proper way. But their emotions are real and authentic just the same. *Also it is critical to understand that the frustration itself may become the subject of a repetitive, persevering behavior, and autistic people might need a little extra time and patience recovering from frustrating issues.*

Since autistic perception is freer from social constraints, it is possible that an autistic person would function within different emotional parameters. In the normal world, people function within the parameters of social pride and social humiliation. In terms of common sense, we associate happiness with pride and sadness with humiliation. But a perception existing outside of these constraints would exist freer of the constraints of social pride and social humiliation. Autistic people may therefore experience more emotional extremes in their daily lives. For example, they may be more prone to experience bliss or grief as a response to an incidental occurrence in their daily lives, whereas a normal person would filter out those extreme responses in an attempt to appear normal.

The circle of light

Imagine you stand in a circle of light, alone in a world of darkness. Imagine that this circle of light is 100 meters in diameter and imagine that this represents your world of perception and emotions. You can't see anything until it enters your circle of light. When some piece of information or some person enters your circle of experience you can see it coming from 50 meters away and you have plenty of time to react.

Now imagine that your circle of light is only 10 meters in diameter in the same world of darkness. Things enter your circle of light and they are upon you immediately almost without notice or warning. You don't have time to process the experience, because as soon as something enters your circle of experience and emotions it is in your face almost immediately.

This is an analogy for comparing normal perception with autistic perception. Normal perception sheds light on incoming data. It makes meaningful sense out of the world. But autistic people simply have a narrower circle of interactive experience. People and information come at them seemingly out of nowhere. There is no forewarning or prospective ability to prepare for the world.

If your normal world is full of light, then you have plenty of understanding and plenty of time to plan and adjust. But in your autistic world the light shines only for you, and anything entering your circle of light feels unannounced and intrusive. You would rather be left alone than constantly having to deal with all of the sensory data and people in the world suddenly appearing out of nowhere to confront you.

People with strong autistic perception have to condescend to negotiate the normal social world. The world is full of demands and expectations that buzz around their heads like so many gnats and mosquitoes. Meanwhile, they take pleasure from the smallest, most inconsequential things. They can watch a piece of jewelry sparkle, and watch, and watch, and watch. They can rock back and forth for long periods of time, and it is a comforting, very automatic experience for them.

There is reason to believe that people with autism are capable of experiencing a wider range of emotions simply because their emotions are not filtered out by social thinking. If this is true, then autistic people are probably capable of experiencing states of bliss and not apt to communicate this to the rest of the world. Left to their own devices, they will enter repetitive states of perception and motion that will deliver them into their own state of mind. A state of mind with comparatively less self, one that has effectively transcended the constraints of the material world – a rather transcendent state of being.

Two-dimensional perception

Autistic perception is more two-dimensional than normal perception, which is more three-dimensional and more generalized. A person with very strong autistic perception will actually have trouble distinguishing between furniture and people. Everything is just one thing. It's a flat world with no discernible characteristics. It's a world where furniture talks. It's a world where people have the significance of straw dogs. This animated two-dimensional world is very much like a cartoon. It's like being in Wonderland. It can be frightening and it can be wonderful. Life inside a fairy tale can be horrific and it can be serene.

I think the thing about autism that bothers us the most is that autistic people don't seem to care about us. It is shocking enough for us to interact with a person who is oblivious to our needs and expectations. But for them not to care on top of it is just plain bewildering.

Another aspect of the lowered filters of social thinking seems to be a higher tolerance for physical pain. It would seem that we actually learn to respond to hot and cold in our childhood socialization as a matter of practicality, and also because we have a brain wired up to filter a normal experience of hot and cold. But there are reports of autistic children who seem completely unaware of being in extreme temperatures. The fact that autistic people just don't have the same boundaries normal people have challenges us. They don't seem to have any boundaries that make sense to us at all.

To this extent, severely autistic people may engage repetitive routines of behavior that would be physically unimaginable to us. But we are now in a position to understand that even awareness of one's own body and oneself is based in social thinking (specifically the ability to see yourself through the eyes of others). So autistic people neither feel their bodies the way a normal person does, nor have awareness of their bodies as a normal person does. It's as if autistic people engage the repetitive routines in order to create a sense of consistency and reality exactly because they can't rely on their bodies for normal cues of consistency and reality.

Since autistic perception is more two-dimensional and controlled by this If-Then theme, autistic people may tend to repeat whatever has been said around them at any given time. This is referred to as echolalia. This is also a part of the mystery of autism, yet it is easily apprehended by us at this point because we know they have less social thinking and relatively more computer thinking. So, without filtering out behavior that goes against social norms of etiquette, an autistic person will innocently and naturally be in a state of mind that mimics the surrounding world. If they hear it, then they will repeat it.

I once heard of an autistic boy who ran around the house screaming every time his parents turned on the vacuum cleaner. This behavior seemed very alarming to the family. I suggested this was echolalia.

Autistic savants

One of the most intriguing phenomena in the world of autism is the ability of the autistic savant. We have all heard of autistic savants who can perform incredible feats of calculation or artistry. Generally, these skills take the following forms:

- calculation and memory – such as reciting the weather for any day in the last century, or being able to say what day of the week any date falls on in the last century

- being able to count with great speed – in the movie *Rain Man* we see a savant looking at toothpicks on the floor and immediately stating how many are there, or another savant I once heard of could run his finger across a clothes rack and immediately state how many hangers were there

- drawing and sculpture – of particular fascination is that these abilities revolve around the ability to replicate any object with amazing, almost perfect, detail

- music – again, these abilities revolve around the ability to hear any piece of music and play it immediately by ear.

Some savant capabilities can be described in terms of super-computer thinking. Other abilities can be understood in terms of If-Then computer thinking. If I see something, then I can draw it the same way I saw it. If I hear something, then I can play it the same way I heard it. In other words, savant capabilities comprise acts of replication. If you give me two apples, then I will give you two apples back.

It also seems that amazing powers of memory go along with high computer thinking. This implies two things. First, that social thinking acts as a filter for all but the most immediate normal concerns. So, with less social thinking, there are fewer filters there to filter out long-term memories. Second, it implies that computer thinking supports long-term memory.

Short-term thinking is all about defining the current social situation. With far less of that available, what's left is the computer thinking and its support of long-term memory. This exists uninhibited by the social thinking so we see autistic people having incredible memories.

Autistic people will tend to recite long passages from a television show or movie with the greatest of ease. In fact, they will enjoy watching that movie over and over again. This brings together the incredible long-term memory that is being supported by the computer thinking without inhibition from the filters of thinking, and the penchant for repetitive behavior. They might watch the same video or movie endlessly. Should this be a cause for concern?

Not necessarily. There is a difference between coaxing an autistic person through gentle persuasion, and getting upset over their behavior. There is no use getting upset about their behavior. If you perceive the need or the opportunity, just engage a patient plan to introduce a new show or movie into their life. If you feel the need to do so, you may be able to teach your autistic child all kinds of things. But, there is no use getting upset over autistic behaviors. Careful and dedicated teachers are conditioning functional behaviors and eliminating disturbing behaviors in their autistic students every day. With perseverance, one If-Then routine for action can be replaced with another.

Autistic people have their own sense of self and may be given to a wide array of talents. They are every bit as unique as any other human being. But, we can probably expect to see their talents and perceptions and behavior running along the lines of activities that require If-Then thinking.

Forget normal expectations

We tend to over-dramatize the behavior of autistic people because we ourselves don't understand it. Once I heard of an autistic boy who would run out of his classroom from time to time. Now at first you might think "Oh no, that kid was probably running all over school like a wild man." But, that was not the case at all. Every time he left he would go to a pile of rocks on the playground on the other side of campus. His teacher would always know to walk over there and find him. Why? Because he loved rocks, and once he found out about that pile of rocks, he would run out of class from time to time and go sit on the pile of rocks and play with the rocks. The point is that this same If-Then kind of thinking even governed his rebellious behavior. Even in his most rambunctious moments he was predictable, and always did the same thing over and over again.

Autistic people tend to want to be left alone. They want to engage their favorite repetitive behaviors. But to indulge this obsessive side of their nature might be an experience of mental health for them. The task for those around them is simply to make sure they are not presenting a danger to self and others. Autistic people may be able to experience great joy and bliss. Likewise, their experience of anxiety and stress comes from being inundated by pressures and expectations of the normal world.

The most important thing is to understand autistic people. We don't have to change them or make them into normal people. We will be much less stressed ourselves if we relinquish the obsession we tend to have with repeating our own normal behaviors.

Even staring should be counted among the repetitive behaviors. It's looking at something over and over again. Sometimes we all lose ourselves in a moment and keep staring at something for an excessively long period of time. If those around us notice, they may think it's funny and enjoy getting us out of this momentary trance-like state. This happened much more when we were younger. I would suggest this was a momentary visit into an autistic state of perception. It was a pleasant experience, although it was not one you could easily share. Remember?

Chapter Four

Three Keys to Communicating with Autistic People

The camp counselor ran into my office. "The autistic kid is freaking out! Call his mother! Tell her to come pick him up! He's got to go!" As the camp director I knew the first thing I had to do was calm the counselor down because he was the one who was freaking out! He said the boy had been disciplined for a minor, and very common, infraction of the rules. But, at that point, the boy had become upset and withdrawn. He began crying, sat down on some steps, and refused to communicate or listen to anyone.

I went to the boy. I told everyone to leave us alone and carry on. The boy's older brother was especially concerned. I told him not to worry, that everything would be fine. Ten minutes later the high-functioning autistic boy rejoined his camp group, and was absolutely fine for the rest of the day.

Anyone can do what I did. What did I do? How did I know what to do? It's really quite simple. While there is a growing body of work from autism experts that is highly informative regarding the application of conditioning techniques for learning and re-learning behaviors, this story stands apart from the application of those techniques. This is a story about persuasion and meaningful communication on the spur of the moment. First, let me tell you exactly what happened between the boy, who we will call Jimmy, and me. Then we will examine in closer detail why it worked.

The story of Jimmy and me

As I joined Jimmy, he was sitting on some steps with a group of kids standing around looking at him. It's amazing how quickly people zoom in on anyone that stands out as different. The first thing I did was sit down next to Jimmy as if nothing had happened. Then I indicated to everybody it was time to resume their normal activity. As it was time for lunch, everybody was scheduled to go inside anyway, and so they left us alone.

Jimmy was sniffling. He had obviously been crying and he was upset. Now this is interesting. He rested his head in the palm of his left hand. And he was tapping the stair with his right hand. It was as if he was keeping the beat or the rhythm for a piece of music. Not too slow, and not too fast. It was just a steady rhythm of about 80 beats per minute.

I began to do the same thing with my left hand. I wasn't particularly trying to match his rhythm 100 per cent, but I was roughly mirroring his tapping of the step. I had my chin resting on the palm of my right hand. There we sat.

After about 15 seconds Jimmy looked over at me. You should have seen the look on his face! His eyebrows were furrowed, and he looked over at me with complete amazement. He didn't make eye contact, but kind of looked at my hand tapping the step, looked me over once, and then went back to his original position. I just looked away. I just kept tapping the step. I would say we sat there together tapping the step for about two minutes.

During those two minutes I stopped tapping the steps once for about ten seconds and then I resumed. And after those two minutes, Jimmy stopped his tapping.

I continued tapping. I tapped for about 30 seconds. Then I stopped for about ten seconds. Then I continued tapping once again for about one minute.

Then Jimmy lifted his head. Looking at a row of pedal cars arranged in the parking lot for the children to ride he said, "That pedal car is blue."

To which I responded, "Yes, Jimmy sees a pedal car that is blue. Would Jimmy like to ride that pedal car?"

He nodded his head yes and we both stood up. We walked over to the car together. Jimmy got in the car and proceeded to drive it around the parking lot. After about two minutes I approached him and said, "I think it's about time for lunch. Would Jimmy like to go inside and maybe have some lunch?"

Jimmy nodded his head yes. We both walked inside. I helped Jimmy get his lunch and I sat him down at a table by himself. He began eating and I figured he was safe and comfortable, so I walked away to attend to some other matters. I was planning on keeping in close touch with him, but I did have other things to do. As the camp director, I had hundreds of children and numerous employees to oversee.

After a few more minutes I turned around to check on him. He was no longer at his table. He was playing with some of the children from his group. I decided to leave well enough alone. The rest of the day proceeded as normal – as if nothing unusual had happened.

Understanding the story of Jimmy and me: The three keys

Now let's take a closer look at exactly why this approach may have worked so well. In so doing we will observe three keys to communicating with autistic people. These three all-important keys are:

1.   *staying calm,* for example by making sure yourself and others are relaxed and supportive

2.   *reflecting their behavior,* for example by mirroring one of their repetitive motions

3.   *reflecting their perception,* for example by referring to them in the third person.

We'll take a closer look at the story of Jimmy and me in terms of the three keys.

Staying calm

I stayed calm. The last thing I was going to do was react in a way that was overly emotional. Autism does not scare me. It does not make me feel uncomfortable. I am not committed to making autistic people act normal all of the time. I don't get upset when autistic people get upset. I don't get upset when normal people get upset. I don't judge autistic people as inferiors that should be removed from the circle of normalcy the moment they have a little trouble with social life. I am autism-friendly. I had known Jimmy for only a couple of days, but his mother had told me that he was academically gifted, and I thought he was a great kid.

My first task was to calm everybody else down. After I arrived on the scene it took about a minute to get everybody calmed down and to convince them that they should leave the area and go inside to have lunch. There was a little scene, and it brought a little excitement into everybody's day. But, I know the normal world and I know how normal people are. The moment we had a child with autism sign up for camp everybody knew about it. People love to talk. It was no surprise to me that this child would be singled out as needing to leave camp before any other child. The rule he had violated was probably the most common rule violation we had to deal with at camp. It was utterly common.

Jimmy's problem was not that he had violated the rules. This part of the story is critically important to recognize. *Jimmy's problem was that he had trouble getting back on track after having been disciplined by the counselor.* Jimmy was angry because the counselor had disciplined him; but instead of getting over it and getting back into the mix of things, Jimmy remained angry. At this point he was scolded for not being a good sport, and now he became even more hurt. All I did was give Jimmy a sense of trust, respect, safety, and comfort based on my understanding of the logic of his perception so that he could take the time he needed to recover from his disciplinary experience and get back into the flow of fun with his peers.

Jimmy just needed a little extra time and understanding. The single greatest obstacle to this was the tendency for others to invoke assumptions of normalcy and become excited and critical of Jimmy. Staying calm is a critical factor in communicating with autistic people.

I spent time with Jimmy alone. This was the lucky part. I was lucky they were all scheduled to go inside and have lunch. I think it was really important for me and Jimmy to have some time alone, away from everybody else. If they had not been scheduled to leave the area, I would have done well to ask the counselor to move the children to another area for a ten-minute break. It might seem to be the reverse of what is normal. It might not seem fair that the normal children should be asked to leave the area in order to help the autistic child get back on track. But is it really too much to ask?

Reflecting their behavior

I reflected Jimmy's repetitive behavior. As soon as I had sat down next to Jimmy and noticed that he had started tapping the step I was thrilled! When you deal with autistic people it is something you can look for with great predictability. You know they will be engaging repetitive behaviors. Furthermore, you know these behaviors will be meaningful to them. It's ironic that normal people are so put off by dealing with autistic people. But the normal point of view is also understandable and predictable. How can you deal with someone when you don't have any idea what is going on in his or her head? How can you deal with someone who won't behave normally, someone who is unpredictable in the normal ways that most people are predictable?

Ironically, autistic people are quite predictable in their own ways, you just have to understand them. As soon as I noticed this repetitive behavior I was thrilled because I had something to hold on to, a bridge that I could use to meet him halfway. Immediately, I began to do the same thing.

Why is it that we are so ready, willing, and able to meet people halfway in order to communicate with them, and so mystified by autistic people? It is simply because we haven't been able to understand them.

If we plan a trip to another country where people speak a foreign language, we might make an attempt to learn how to say a few phrases in that language so we can communicate with the people there. It's fun to do this and we know it might help smooth out the trip. We might learn some of their customs for the same reason. It's the heart and soul of diplomacy that you meet people halfway by reflecting their perception and behavior, their language and their customs. It's the same thing with autistic people. When you know to look for them, it's fun to watch for their repetitive behaviors.

I did this in an interactive and sympathetic way with Jimmy. I didn't make a big deal out of it. I didn't stare at him the whole time I was doing it. I didn't say a word to him. I simply joined him. With autistic people, sometimes the way to show support and affiliation is by leaving them alone. In other words, the last thing I wanted to do was be intrusive. I simply wanted to reflect his behavior.

The strange look on his face indicated to me that he wasn't accustomed to this. He didn't expect it. But, he was fine with it. It was the single best way for me to communicate to him that I understood him and I was on his side.

While Jimmy was tapping the step, somehow I sensed that I should stop tapping for a moment and then start again. Somehow I sensed that I should keep tapping after he stopped. Somehow I sensed that I should stop tapping and then start tapping one more time, even though he had already stopped his tapping. I sensed all of this because I was trying to communicate with him and then coax him back into the normal world. The idea was not to sit there tapping all day. The idea was to pick up with the repetitive behavior and slowly ease back into the normal world.

Because I knew to reflect Jimmy's behavior I was able to give him a way to identify with me. This allowed him to begin recovering his sense of trust, respect, safety, and comfort.

Reflecting their perception

I referred to Jimmy in the third person, instead of the second person. Since I know that autistic people often refer to themselves in the third person, I decided to do the same thing. This was a critical means of reflecting his perception back to him. It was another way of meeting him halfway. Since autistic people have less social thinking compared to their computer thinking, less ability to see themselves through the eyes of others, and therefore less of an ability to experience a full-blown interactive self, they tend to refer to themselves in the third person. So, I also referred to Jimmy in the third person.

Instead of saying, "Yeah, that's a blue pedal car" I said, "Yes, Jimmy sees a blue pedal car." Instead of saying, "Do you want to ride the blue pedal car?" I said, "Does Jimmy want to ride the blue pedal car?" Instead of saying, "Do you want to eat lunch?" I said, "Does Jimmy want to eat lunch?"

This manner of speaking was less invasive, less intrusive. I was speaking to him on his level. By reflecting his tapping of the step and then speaking to him in the third person about himself, I was able to make friends with him easily. I was disarming and sympathetic on a deep level. It is important to understand that this was much more than just being nice to him.

By referring to him in the third person I was reflecting his own perception of himself. This was another way of helping him to identify with me. It also helped him to feel comfortable with me. This was a systematic bridge-building exercise I was able to engage based on my understanding of social and computer thinking. Anyone can do the same thing.

I gently coaxed him back into the group. The goal of my interaction was to give Jimmy a human experience of trust, respect, safety, and comfort. It is critically important to understand that his biggest problem was the inability to receive discipline, acknowledge it, and then return to normal activity. This is all part of being normal, but he had trouble getting back on track. We should not be surprised that less social thinking should lead to more trouble getting back on track in the normal world.

If you were autistic, how would you want people to communicate with you?

Normal people tend to think that communication needs to be forced with autistic people. I once saw a teacher of autistic children reduced to grabbing the hands of an autistic child, looking at him nose to nose, and yelling, "You can't do that!" That might be a normal reaction to an abnormal situation, but nothing normal is really going to help us much when it comes to understanding autism.

There is a difference between trying to force communication and trying to meet somebody halfway. When dealing with an autistic person we would be better off relinquishing our own assumptions of normalcy and catering to their needs. We somehow assume that communication and education for autistic people will serve to help make them more normal. But is that necessarily the best way to approach communication with an autistic person?

If we can see that an autistic person is lower on social thinking and higher on the computer, then we need to pick up from there and start finding ways to meet them halfway instead of continually seeing the goal as the full or even partial normalization of the child. It will be difficult for us to imagine that we might create a different educational agenda for people with autism. Autism is so confusing to normal people. It is confusing to see a child who can perform certain intellectual feats while at the same time being unable to do the simplest things using common sense.

It's easy for us to assume that if a child can learn to point to the signboard, then they can learn proper manners. But that child who is so strongly autistic as to be nonverbal is able to learn to use the signboard because it conforms to If-Then rules for action. They are unable to learn proper manners because they have relatively less social thinking, and manners are social commodities.

It's easy for us to imagine that if a child can learn to read well, then they can learn to accept discipline and get back on track as soon as possible. But, the social graces will tend to elude such a person, no matter how great their intellectual feats.

Our system of education and our entire society are based on a combination of intellectual learning and social graces. We always assume that the two have to go together. We have a lot of trouble seeing someone who can get one and not the other. But if our perception is made up of social and computer thinking, then we should make allowances for the notion that these areas of capability might also exist quite separately of one another.

You might ask if we could use If-Then thinking to establish rules for action that conform to manners and social graces. On the one hand, that is the principal dynamic of classical conditioning exercises that are often used with success. But the other side of the coin is that the autistic person will always have trouble generalizing these rules while moving from one social situation to another.

Autistic people tend to take things literally. They have trouble embellishing perception with assumptions of normalcy. Consider the autistic girl who became upset when the doctor asked her to give him her hand. He just wanted to take her pulse, but she thought he wanted her to remove her hand and give it to him. Things are taken literally. Everything is If-Then and there is little room for making assumptions of normalcy or generalizing about how normal people might see this or react to that.

There was an autistic boy who loved to watch *Star Wars* over and over again. One day he became upset when his mother wanted to stop the movie, and take him to the store with her. He thought that Luke Skywalker would not be saved if he didn't finish watching the movie. For him the If-Then sequence was "If the movie is watched, then the hero will be saved."

So, it's one thing to condition autistic children to do this or that, but it is another to expect them to generalize their knowledge in the outside world. Some people with autistic perception experience a great amount of normalization on their own as they mature through life. But, this is not something that can be forced with classical conditioning exercises.

We are now in a position to begin taking an autism-friendly, sympathetic approach to understanding autism and meeting autistic people halfway.

Any teacher who spends time working with autistic children deserves a medal. Any parent who bends over backwards to advocate for his or her child deserves the complete respect and support of the entire society. Anybody who tries to take advantage of the culture of autism by parading miracle cures or discoveries ought to be ashamed of themselves.

There was a controversy once upon a time surrounding a technique called facilitated communication. It was claimed that if the facilitator simply touched the elbow of the autistic child, this enabled the child to type in ways that revealed the normal person within. As soon as I saw examples of facilitated communication in which the autistic children spoke in the first person with great fluency I was suspicious. Is it really possible for children with strong autistic perception to write fluently in the first person when describing themselves? Seemingly, lesser social thinking leads to lesser self, and these children will tend to communicate about themselves in the third person. I don't think touching someone's elbow would change the way his or her brain is wired up for perception and behavior.

The more we understand autism, the better we are able to communicate and understand what autistic people can do and what they can't do. If we adopt this picture of autism as supported by computer thinking that is higher than social thinking, we will begin to clear up many of the mysteries that have surrounded the world of autism. As soon as we understand that computer thinking will tend to repeat itself again and again, we have a great insight. As soon as we understand that the filters of social thinking are loosened, we will understand that autistic people are capable of meaningful, human experience that exists within a very tight circle of perception.

A good example of this is the autistic sense of humor. Yes, autistic people are capable of laughing and smiling. They are capable of having a great sense of humor. But we shouldn't be too surprised if the autistic person tells the same joke or story over and over and over again. We shouldn't be too surprised if they laugh at the same thing again and again and again. We can therefore expect autistic people to laugh in a way that is also not quite normal. Maybe they will laugh too loud, or too long. They just won't gauge normalcy when they think something is funny. I was once a member of an autism discussion group on the internet in which two high-functioning autistic people shared the same joke and story with one another every day as if they had never done it before.

As the filters of social thinking are lowered we can also expect autistic people to be hypersensitive. Normal social thinking is like a buffer that filters out most of the world, leaving only what serves a normal social function. But autistic people live outside of that world and actually perceive more sensory data in finer and finer gradations than do normal people. That is why they can be hypersensitive to certain sounds, or lights, or fabrics. Any of the senses can be affected in this way.

We need to understand autistic people and to try to help them understand the normal world as much as possible. Once we have established rapport, using If-Then statements as much as possible may be of some help. For example, an autistic child may not grasp the idea that other people have feelings. We can say to that child, "If you do this, it might make someone unhappy and that is not good." We can begin to build on this by saying, "If you are good, then I will give you a piece of candy. If you are not good, then you will not get a piece of candy." The only reason there has been any success at all teaching behavior modification to autistic children is because these programs are based on If-Then rules for action. Find out how much comprehension the child has of If-Then statements and work from there on that level.

In a way, what I am saying is that instead of trying only to make autistic people behave normally, we will all have to understand autism a little better and behave a little more autistically ourselves. "When in Rome, do as the Romans do" is the old saying. And when you want to communicate with an autistic person you might as well understand computer thinking as well as possible and start from there.

Chapter Five

How We Are All Autistic to One Extent or Another

At that same camp described in Chapter 4, the word had spread quickly that we had an autistic child enrolled. One day one of the camp counselors nudged my shoulder. He leaned over and pointed to a boy saying, "That kid is autistic."

"What?" I asked with surprise.

"That kid right over there, he's the kid with autism," he said as if he were conveying a secret.

"No, he's not," I smiled. "It's that one over there!"

This was fascinating to me. There is a lot going on in that little story. First of all, in the normal world anyone who stands out is not only labeled, but actively searched out by normal members in good standing. It is almost an obligation of normal members to pass the word around so that everyone knows who is who. In the normal world it is extremely important that we all know who we are.

But in this little example the fact is that the counselor had made an erroneous assumption. He had identified a child as being autistic who was actually not autistic! Furthermore, our high-functioning autistic friend Jimmy had passed as normal in that counselor's eyes! So what is going on in this normal world anyway?

If you could spend a little time with Jimmy you would recognize that his perception and behavior are not quite normal. You would have to address him in a louder tone of voice to get his attention sometimes. The most incidental things would fascinate him. But at the same time, it is entirely possible that Jimmy might pass as normal in the eyes of plenty of people, plenty of the time.

One of the fascinating aspects of learning to understand autism is that we will actually have a new understanding of everyone. We will have a new and powerful way of understanding all human perception. More than just being nice to autistic people, this book challenges everyone to take a new view on all human perception. The result is that understanding autism will enhance the understanding we have of ourselves and of all human experience.

Every once in a while, as I am explaining social and computer thinking and how it relates to autism, some smart person will ask me, "If this is true, then aren't we all autistic?" Bingo! The most perceptive people quickly tune into the notion that there is a little bit of autism in all of us. Let's take a closer look at how this works.

Normalcy and repetitive behaviors

If computer thinking is the essence of autistic thinking, and if computer thinking is a part of everyone's perception, then the essence of autism lies within everyone's perception. It's really a question of how much the social thinking balances out the computer thinking. If computer thinking is higher than social thinking, then we will tend to see the characteristics of autism emerge. If social thinking is higher than computer thinking, then the autistic traits will be overshadowed by wonderfully social and interactive traits. But in either case the computer thinking is there calculating behaviors over and over again with amazing predictability.

The normal world is a social and interactive world that is completely based in repetitive behaviors! Remember the analogy of the circle of light? A normal person stands in a larger circle of light than an autistic person. This implies that his or her experience is more generalized. A normal person can tune into the concept of a general public more easily than an autistic person. A normal person has a wider bandwidth, a more generalized experience, and their repetitive routines will simply take place on a daily, weekly, or yearly basis.

Normalcy as the generalization of autism

Social thinking balances out computer thinking and generalizes computer thinking to conform to the functions of social thinking. But, social thinking is still utterly dependent upon computer thinking. If a person had normal social thinking and zero computer thinking, they would not be able to compute behavior. They would likely just sit there with a smile on their face, taking it all in, happy to see other people, but completely unable to behave or even move in any meaningful way at all. In fact, there is a rare form of dementia called Pick's disease that conforms to this profile.

Instead of seeing normalcy as the opposite of autism, we should see it as a generalization of autism. Instead of seeing autistic people as completely different than normal people, we should see them as incredibly more focused than normal people.

Social institutions

The entire social world is completely organized in terms of If-Then rules for action. It's not only computer programs that are built using If-Then rules for action, it is all social institutions, all cultures, and everything you and I do all day long.

Let's take greeting rituals, for example. If somebody greets you, then you are supposed to greet them in reciprocal fashion. Let's say I meet somebody I know and they smile and say, "Hey, Alex, what's up?" At that point I have to respond with something that matches, and follows through, and complements that greeting. If I just look at them like they have three eyes and turn around and walk away they will either be offended or they will doubt my sanity.

This is a law of social life that carries all the power of gravity. If somebody I know greets me, then I have to greet them as well. If you don't believe it, just try going through one entire day without responding appropriately to greetings. Even if you do this to prove that you can, you will still have to explain yourself later on to all the people you offended. If you don't explain yourself later, those people may never look at you the same way again. This is a simple yet very powerful example of the way If-Then rules for action control and define our social lives.

We all have habits. Some are good, some are not so good. But all habits are based in If-Then rules for action. If I have just woken up in the morning, then I will brush my teeth and fix my hair. Try breaking that rule for a few days. Your very sanity is at stake here, especially regarding the way other people see you and judge you. Try not brushing your teeth, not fixing your hair, and not greeting anyone properly for a week. You will be treated like you are a menace to society.

Some people have If-Then habits such as "If I am waking up in the morning, then I must drink coffee and read the newspaper." Once we get locked into these habits of action it is difficult to get out of them. It takes a concerted effort to relinquish our habits of action. If we wake up one morning and there is no coffee or no newspaper, we will probably get upset.

So you see the point: we are all locked into repetitive, persevering behaviors! The difference between an autistic person and a normal person is that normal people have repetitive, persevering behaviors that are simply more generalized. Instead of engaging the repetitive behavior at any time of the day, the normal person might engage the behavior at the same general time every day, or at the same time every week. We have a repetitive, persevering behavior enacted on a weekly basis in the normal world that is very special to many of us – it's called the weekend.

Try forcing any normal person to stop their repetitive behaviors – you will get a reaction quite similar to that of trying to stop an autistic person from their repetitive behaviors. The difference is that the autistic person seems oblivious to the time of day or the demands of the social situation. The autistic person cares far less what other people think. Whereas both normal and autistic people engage repetitive behaviors based in this If-Then logic, normal people care much more automatically about what other people think.

The computer thinking gives rise to repetitive behaviors that seem obsessive. But, surely no one can deny that normal people love their obsessions, too. Whether it's watching their favorite sport on television, or looking forward to watching their favorite television show at the same time, same channel, next week, normal people are just as guilty of obsessive behavior as any autistic person. It's just that they engage their obsessions in rather generalized, social ways. Normal people like to share their obsessions, while autistic people would rather be left alone.

The entire concept of social institutions rests on these If-Then rules for action. In education it's "If you want to gain admission to this college, then you have to do the following things." In law it's "If you break this law, then you will be institutionalized." In the family it's "If you want to get married, then you have to do these things." In business it's "If you want to succeed, then you have to attend to the bottom line."

There is simply no way that society itself could exist without laying down firm and clear If-Then rules for action. We like to tell the story of how these rules have changed over time. When we tell this story we call it "history." And when someone wants to change the rules all by themselves we call them a rebel, or an outlaw, or an anarchist.

One of the most powerful aspects of American culture is the generalized routine we have for holding elections every two years and every four years. And nobody in the USA would even think of questioning why we change time itself on a regular basis. We spring forward an hour every spring, and fall back one hour in the fall, year in and year out, even though people have generally forgotten why. We tend to take these things for granted, but these are all examples of the way our lives are governed by If-Then rules for action.

If I see a stop sign, then I will stop. If I see a green light, then I will go. It's almost funny the way we look at autistic people and let ourselves be completely confused by the way they get stuck in repetitive actions.

In fact, normal people are obsessively stuck on repeating the behaviors of the normal world. And to attempt to get them to stop is to invite an emotional backlash. That's why normal people have so much trouble accepting autistic people. Autistic people don't conform to the rather rigid expectations of the normal world. The reason normal people get upset when autistic people engage repetitive behaviors is because they are not repeating the normal behaviors that have been agreed upon by normal people in the normal world.

Mechanization

One of the most critical aspects of the industrial revolution was the way humans began to mechanize the world. The industrial revolution is understood to signal the beginning of the modern world. Yet what is mechanization but the application of If-Then rules? The entire industrialized world depends on the mechanization of processes and forces of production.

One of the greatest revelations of mechanization is the assembly line. It is said that Henry Ford's vision of building automobiles on an assembly line was his greatest insight. It allowed automobiles to be built more efficiently and cheaply. It allowed for the mass production of automobiles. The assembly line is realized by streamlining production and reducing it to its most essential If-Then rules for action. Whenever the concept of the assembly line has been applied to a product it has produced a revolution. When the concept of assembly-line production was applied to food, it created fast food and McDonald's, and the world has never been the same since. Herbert Simon even received a Nobel Prize in economics for saying that all production systems are based in a series of If-Then rules for action.

In this way, we can see mechanization and assembly-line production as the imposition of computer thinking on the social world. Computer thinking has formulated the modern economy and lies at the heart of our greatest forms of economic production. The logic of computer thinking lies at the heart of our social institutions, our economy of mass production, and our computers themselves.

Bureaucracy

One of the social outcomes of our industrial society has been the appearance of the full-blown bureaucracy. In a bureaucracy, organization is efficiently transformed into a pyramid of power based in written rules. This is powerful, as it underlies the forms of modern corporations. It is also a source of aggravation and stress. This is because bureaucracies tend to feel impersonal.

But we can understand the impersonal nature of the bureaucracy when we come to see it as an organization based in If-Then rules. The human organization functions more like a machine than a person. So, when we get to the place of business one minute late, it is frustrating to see people inside who won't let us in, because if it's closing time, then it's closing time. We are trying to find ways to humanize the bureaucracy as we move into the 21st century, but we can't deny the power of imposing If-Then rules for action on an entire human organization.

The most striking example of bureaucracy is the military forces. Everything in military life is based in a strict adherence to If-Then rules for action. Military life is carved out of an endless sequence of If-Then rules for action. So, in a sense, computer thinking lies at the heart of our most powerful social organizations.

The bureaucracy of science is based in as much computer thinking as possible. Everything about science represents a championing of computer thinking. That is why science itself seems to represent cold and inhuman aspects of human nature. Science stands on the outside looking in on the normal world, and constantly developing and applying If-Then rules for action everywhere it can.

The entire science of mathematics is nothing but the formalization of If-Then rules for action. This concept of formalization is something that comes with computer thinking. To formalize anything means to reduce it to its most basic If-Then rules for action. No matter how much we resent a particular social institution, or bureaucracy, or scientific worldview, we can't deny the seductive power of reducing the world to If-Then rules for action. Computer thinking is the pivot point for progress and success in our lives. In this sense, the integration of social and computer thinking is at the heart of our world today. It is what makes us as sophisticated as we are as a society. The difference between ancient society and modern society lies in this integration of social and computer thinking into all of our social processes.

Instead of assuming that normal people and autistic people are nothing alike, we can learn to see more and more of each in the other. In fact, much of this book has been dedicated to using the person with rather strong autistic perception as the case in point, but let's not forget that the pictures we looked at in the first chapter suggest there is a long continuum of autistic perception. There are plenty of people in society who are higher on the computer than the social. You might be one of them. Let's take a look at the ways we can identify autistic perception at work in the normal world.

Slight autism in the normal world

First, let me state that there seems to be no way to say one talent or behavior holds true for all people that are higher on the computer than the social. Some are good at math, some are not. Some like music, some do not. Some are talented in sports, some are not. If you want to talk about people that are not obviously diagnosable as autistic, but nevertheless higher on the computer than the social, you can't generalize about any traits. The only thing you can generalize about is a reluctance to participate in normal social life in normal ways, and a predilection for obsessive routines.

Some of these people will be successful and happy. Some will be alienated and miserable. Then again, some will be alienated and happy. And some will be successful and miserable. The only thing these people will have in common is a magnetic pull away from normal social routines, as well as marked tendencies toward repetitive behaviors.

Some of the more obvious candidates for this status include homeless people. We tend to assume that homeless people are just strange or irresponsible. But there is a strong possibility that a person who is higher on the computer will be more likely to become homeless and stay that way. I have met homeless people who have made a career out of being homeless, and they are proud of it. This brings us back to the image of a person who is high enough on the social thinking to escape "diagnosis," but the higher computer thinking becomes a pivot point for eccentricity.

I once met a homeless man who explained to me his routine for living – his life was completely structured. He explained to me with pride how well-structured his routines were and told me that for many years he had been playing out these exact same routines for survival with great success. He even communicated to me how he viewed normal people through eyes of condescension. To me, this man was obviously higher on the computer than the social thinking. Nevertheless, there was nothing obviously or diagnosably autistic about him and we had a long friendly conversation.

Once, I knew of a man who spent a one-week vacation from work in his home all by himself cross-referencing his entire collection of records and CDs. By the time he was finished he could look up any artist in his collection and see the albums on which that artist appeared. His collection consisted of over 2500 records and CDs! This image of a man who was not diagnosable as autistic, but preferred to spend his vacation in this way fussing over his collection, is an excellent example of slight autism. He was using his creative computer thinking to create another level of If-Then programming in his collection. "If I look up an artist, then I can see all the albums on which they appear." Furthermore, what would have been an onerous task for another person was actually fun and restful for him. It was a vacation that was truly good for his mental health.

It seems that in Alaska there is a preponderance of children being diagnosed with autism. My guess is that people who are higher on the computer will tend to move to Alaska in the first place, because they want to get away from it all. These people, in turn, will tend to give birth to children who are higher on computer thinking.

The same thing is true of Silicon Valley. We can't be too surprised to find many people who are good at computers and math who are also higher on the computer thinking than the social. But, I want to be very quick to point out that just because someone is higher on the computer does not necessarily mean they will be good at computers and math.

Academics will tend to be higher on the computer also. But, that doesn't mean everyone in academia is autistic. It just implies that for people who are higher on the computer, the ivory tower of academia offers a buffer from the normal world that can be very inviting.

We can start to imagine how the popular myth that genius is close to madness has been proffered over the years. Whether it's the brilliant artist who can't get along with anyone, or the brilliant chess player who becomes a recluse, people who are higher on the computer will tend to stand out as intellectually gifted and socially challenged at the same time. These people will play the game of normal life to a point, but they will not necessarily be very popular.

Another tendency of people who are somewhat normal on the social and much higher on the computer is toward self-medication and addictive behavior. Antidepressants like Prozac are relatively new. But, slightly autistic perception has always been around. People who have trouble fitting into the normal social scene may tend to experience anxiety leading to depression.

Before antidepressants existed, these people may have easily slipped into alcohol or drug abuse in an effort to medicate away the effects of anxiety experienced by always trying to put the square peg of their perception into the round hole of society. The tendency toward repetitive, obsessive behavior kicks in and then they have a problematic routine on their hands.

A person with high computer thinking may not be diagnosed as autistic because their social thinking is normal or above normal. But they may be diagnosed with obsessive-compulsive disorder. For that matter, they might be diagnosed as having an anxiety disorder, depression, or agoraphobia.

I'm not saying that everyone who receives these diagnoses is high on the computer. And I'm not saying everyone who is high on the computer will receive these diagnoses. I'm just saying that people who are higher on the computer will have a tendency to exhibit behaviors that end up being diagnosed this way. Put it this way, almost anybody who had a choice would prefer not to be sick or labeled as abnormal. I think most people who end up that way can't help it. In other words, if you had their brain and their social circumstances you might just as easily end up the same way.

Increasing the circle of light

It is time for us to take a positive, proactive, asset approach to autism. It is too easy to take a negative, medicalized deficit approach. The normal world tends automatically to label anyone who is not normal as deficient and less than desirable. The normal world has to grow and mature before it can accept what is new and different. The gut reaction to autism has been negative historically. But there are many cases of segments of society who were misunderstood and have recently begun to receive acceptance and understanding in the normal world. I am confident that the same thing will happen with autism. As we begin to see ourselves more and more in terms of social and computer thinking, we will begin to identify more and more with autistic people.

This is undoubtedly happening already and we will begin to become more and more aware of it. This is the reason we are so fascinated with Mr. Spock and Data in *Star Trek*. They represent the autistic side in all of us. This is the reason we enjoy *Rain Man* and the increasing number of movies produced by Hollywood featuring autistic people as the stars of the show.

Deep down inside we know that we all share the same essence of humanity. We all share social and computer thinking integrating to create our perception. And since there are probably few people with identical levels of social and computer thinking, we each have our own integration issue before us as well. As we begin to see ourselves in autistic people, and computer thinking in our greatest social achievements, we will begin to integrate the normal world with the autistic world. Autism is a part of the normal world, and the circle of light is growing.

Chapter Six

The Practical Side of Undertanding Autism
Tips for Teaching and Interacting with Autistic People

If a person who is high on the computer thinking becomes interested in a subject, they will easily become obsessed with it, and they will engage the subject with great enthusiasm. If they are not interested in the subject it could be extremely difficult to motivate them. I don't think this is very different from teaching or training anyone else though. But like so many other aspects of autism, this is more exaggerated than with normal people. Generally speaking, most people who are higher on the computer will evidence intellectual abilities in one or more areas. These abilities will often be above average. But let's start this general discussion referring to people with strong autistic perception and then move to high-functioning autism. Lastly we will address the case of people who are high level slightly autistic though not diagnosable as being autistic in contemporary terms.

Teaching and interacting with severely autistic people

The question that is perhaps most critical revolves around the assumed goals for the educational experience of severely autistic people. If the goal is to have a normal experience with the autistic person, then experience will be fraught with frustration and failure. If the goal is to enable the individual to perform as many functional life skills as possible, then the experience is likely to be slow but rewarding. However, if the goal is to enhance the meaningful experience of the autistic person while at the same time learning some functional life skills, then the results are likely to be rewarding, unpredictable, and fulfilling.

In a sense, the biggest challenge to the education of severely autistic people lies in assumptions of normalcy we bring to the experience ourselves. In order to fully understand this statement we ought to reconsider the assumptions of normalcy that lie at the heart of education in the first place. Once we have reached an understanding of the assumptions that support normal education we will be able to understand the need to reexamine our assumed goals for the education of severely autistic individuals.

The social function of education

There is one baseline function that permeates the fabric of all educational institutions. That is simply to socialize children for normal and economically productive behavior in society. That's it. If you consider this for a moment, you will begin to see that by trying to force autistic children to participate in a normal educational experience we are laying the foundation for a questionable experience.

There is nothing more normal than going to school – for a normal child. Part of the power of normalcy is the way normal people take things for granted. These assumptions of normalcy have given rise to our innocent desire to educate people with severely autistic perception. There are few things more automatic than the desire to place a child in school. There are few things more important than enabling our children to have growth experiences in school. But the reason is not strictly that our children need to learn to read and write. The reason is that children need to be socialized to participate in social processes as normal people, and it is simply part of society's survival function to do this.

Sociologically speaking, the purpose and function of education is to socialize children for normal behavior. It is common sense that tells us children go to school to learn to read and write. What more and more people are beginning to realize is that the foundation for reading, writing, and all other intellectual and scholarly work comes from home. Specifically, it comes from one or both parents. Generally, a child's intellectual aptitude is governed and shaped by his or her early childhood interactions with supportive family members. Those children who wait to begin learning how to read and write until they go to school will always tend to be behind those who have the privilege of beginning to learn at home before they ever set foot in a school.

There are more and more children being homeschooled every year. Homeschooling is a new phenomenon that is simply the rediscovery of the oldest truth – a child's learning and enrichment begins in the home. After considering these brief points, we ought to be able to reconsider the purpose of school. Instead of learning how to engage scholarly or intellectual life, school is really all about socialization.

In some sense, the very nature of socialization itself demands that a child must leave the home. In order to become a normally functioning, economically productive member of society, one has to leave the home and go out into the world. Out in the world there will be all kinds of situations that present themselves with all kinds of demands. In order to make sure that children are prepared for this, we have to socialize them. Socialization is how a society ensures that its members can do things together, can work together as a team.

Probably the most important things we all learn to do in school are to sit down together, listen together, take orders together, ask a question by raising our hand first, and then get up and leave together. These simple skills set the stage for us to participate in society for the rest of our lives together. These simple skills prepare us to work together. If a person can't engage this simple skill set, then we have significant challenges to face. I say "we" because we are all somehow implicated in the care and education of everyone in our society. But the entire process of educating children with autism must be seen as qualitatively different than any other kind of education.

Now, if you consider the notion that school exists primarily to fulfill the function of socialization, and if you consider the notion that the skill set of a fully socialized individual is utterly social and interactive, then exactly where does that leave the severely autistic individual when it comes to school and education?

Somehow, we never really have asked ourselves this question as a society. This is probably because we didn't understand autism fully enough to come to terms with the highly constrained nature of severely autistic perception. Somehow, in our liberal, politically correct zeal, we took it upon ourselves several years ago in the United States to mainstream everyone with developmental disabilities. It sounds nice. But it might be upsetting to children with autism to be placed in a public environment! There is simply little use in placing all human beings in a traditional classroom environment and expecting them all to become socialized.

A person with severely autistic perception won't get it. They will never understand the goals and issues of socialization. They won't be able to perform and live up to the expectations of normal school. People with severely autistic perception need a different approach altogether. To place them in classrooms surrounded by teachers and students who don't understand autism is dysfunctional. It's not fair to the person with severely autistic perception, it's not fair to the teachers, and it's not fair to the other students. I once heard of a classroom situation in which an autistic boy mainstreamed into a regular classroom had been positioned by the teacher so he was sitting in the back of the room with his desk facing toward the window, away from the other students. Obviously, this student's educational experience was at cross-purposes with the normal students' educational experience.

People with severe autistic perception deserve to be in surroundings with privacy, not crowded school settings. A crowded school setting will put them on edge and further frustrate whatever educational experience is possible. These people need private, one-on-one coaching with teachers who are trained to work with autistic children.

Preventing teacher burnout

At the same time, since the nature of teaching children with autism is so challenging, principals of schools should also make sure that the teachers themselves are taken care of, and not ignored. Burnout is caused from the aggravation of not being able to control one's destiny at work. In other words, it is not caused by hard work alone. Burnout is brought on by stress, and stress is brought on by challenges to our meaningful perception. So, the two key factors in ensuring the ongoing success and fulfillment of teachers of children with autism are:

1. teachers must understand the nature of autistic perception so as to avoid using normal standards for themselves or the students

2. teachers must receive the full support of the principal of their school.

The principal of the school will be the strongest ally of the teachers of children with autism. For example, a principal might go out of his or her way to make sure that teachers of autistic children are given a day off from time to time in order to attend support groups or informative workshops. These days would be a break in the pace, and they would also be supportive and instructional. If anyone ever complains about teachers of autism getting more days off than other teachers, if anyone questions the notion of these teachers getting special treatment, all they need to do is spend 15 minutes in the classroom with one of these teachers and they will leave with a new appreciation. In other words, being autism-friendly ought to include elite treatment for teachers of children with autism as well.

In such settings, teachers can work on conditioning exercises that will begin to effect changes and growth in the behavior of the severely autistic individual. But the most important aspect of this experience should not be the education of the autistic children. If education is for socialization, then education is not for a child who is severely autistic. The implication is that the teaching experience should revolve around the creature comfort of the autistic child. Specifically, the teaching experience should revolve around finding and establishing functional and enjoyable repetitive routines for the autistic child.

The challenge should be understood in terms of creature comfort as opposed to socialization. There is a big difference between saying the goal of education is to achieve some kind of normal socialization, and saying the goal of this teaching experience is to ensure the creature comfort of this autistic child. In point of fact, these two goals are at odds with one another. We support one to the detriment of the other.

Again and again, the education of severely autistic people is treated like the staging of a tragic play. Behind closed doors teachers talk about educating these children as if it were a tragic experience. Often, teaching assistants are employed to help the special education teachers. But these people will not have as much education as the full-fledged teacher. Though they are a great source of support in classrooms for children with developmental disabilities, they themselves may suffer from burnout if they do not have the privilege of approaching their position with as much understanding as possible. There is a tremendous amount of stress and frustration associated with the education of severely autistic children. Consequently the burnout rate for these teachers is high. *But, the high burnout rate is almost inevitable considering the way we approach the situation in the first place.* In other words, while we are working to make great strides improving the educational experience of children with autism we ought to be equally concerned with making great strides reducing burnout among teachers of children with autism, as well as among their assistants. The key to doing so is reexamining our current assumptions and understandings regarding autism.

The education of a severely autistic child is a tragic experience when it is viewed against the backdrop of normalcy. It becomes a source of frustration if it is held up to all the traditional standards of normalcy. A teacher of autistic children who is on the verge of burnout will feel as though they have to keep going through the motions, even though at the end of the day they're not sure why.

For example, what if the goal of severely autistic children's education would become the development of functional routines for survival, and the development of safe routines for creature comfort? The world of education for autism would change dramatically. There are many teachers and hard-working teacher assistants who enter the classroom every day feeling as though their plight is never going to be fulfilled. They will be spending one more day trying to find some ways to help that autistic student do something that appears normal. But if their goal would now become reasonable and possible to accomplish, teachers and students would be released from a tremendous amount of stress and anxiety. To impose the standards and goals of normal socialization on autistic children and their teachers is not necessarily wise.

Teachers experience burnout when they are held up to normal expectations, which they will never be able to achieve. Instead of trying to find ways to simulate a normal educational experience for children with autism, why not approach autism on its own terms? If the education of an autistic child is set apart from normal educational processes, the experience could become completely rewarding. A teacher will only experience burnout when they feel as though their work will never be appreciated in the normal world.

When teachers find themselves in classroom situations they must begin their approach from a position of understanding. Since each autistic person is an individual, the teacher must spend time observing that individual as well as interacting with parents in order to learn as much as possible about that person.

But a person who really understands autism will take on this challenge with enthusiasm because they have an edge. A teacher who understands autism will know what to look for, before they ever meet their student. They will walk into the teacher–student relationship knowing what questions to ask. What are their favorite repetitive routines? What hypersensitivity might be experienced? Is it to sound, or light, or touch? What do they like the most? What do they dislike the most?

Suspend your assumptions of normalcy. Did you know some autistic people enjoy putting jigsaw puzzles together upside-down? What kind of a mind would enjoy putting a jigsaw puzzle together face down? It is important to allow the autistic child room to express their likes and talents. Who knows what will transpire?

This approach is completely different than a normal approach. It is nothing like saying "Okay, let's see if I can get this kid to act normal." Forget about normal. Remember that person does not stand in a circle of light that is 100 meters in diameter. They may stand in a circle of light that is closer to 10 meters in diameter. So, the teacher will want to take their time approaching the student. The teacher will want to effect a very gentle approach.

Perhaps one of the greatest ironies is that the teacher will encourage intimacy by leaving the child alone. This seems ridiculous. But the severely autistic person does not engage relationships like normal people. With autistic people intimacy is something that will exist by virtue of keeping one's social distance. For example, let the child understand that you are not intrusive or intimidating. Help them to enjoy what they like the most, and then leave them alone for periods of time. Slowly move into their circle of light taking as much time as possible to do it.

This may seem to an unenlightened person like doing nothing. But given our understanding of autism, this is actually doing everything right. You might actually establish a relationship with an autistic person by virtue of the fact that they become accustomed to engaging repetitive routines with this person who knows how to leave them alone and help them to enjoy themselves in a comfortable fashion.

It should not be hard for us at this point to understand that autistic people have difficulty with basic social behaviors like looking someone else in the eye, shaking hands, touching, hugging, and even standing in long lines. As social thinking gets lower and lower in comparison to computer thinking, we also find that the functions of social thinking are weaker and weaker, and the filters of social thinking start to drop away. You will recall that social thinking is responsible for supporting our sense of self.

This derives from the third function of social thinking, the ability to see yourself through the eyes of others. You have to see yourself as a social object, the same way other people see you as a social object, in order to fully objectify yourself to yourself. It's almost as if you have to move into another person's head in your imagination, and imagine how they are seeing you. Then you have to be able to come back full circle into your own head, recover that other person's perception, and resolve it with your own. You actually have to be able to do all this in order to have the experience of being yourself, or talking to yourself.

Now, in autistic perception this will take place less and less the stronger the autistic perception. This means that autistic people will not have as much of a sense of self, and that ultimately means they will have less awareness of their own bodies.

The act of self-awareness is essentially grounded in the ability to locate one's own body in a social situation. The stronger the autistic perception the more difficult this is to do. Consequently, we find severely autistic people having considerable difficulty learning and doing anything that requires awareness of their own bodies. It does not occur to us on the level of common sense that the same perception that has trouble with social issues will also have trouble recognizing itself and, specifically, recognizing its own body.

The resulting perception and experience is something that is downright surreal. But, as soon as we understand this it explains more mysteries of autism. For example, children with very strong autistic perception will take much, much longer to be toilet trained. It simply takes them much, much longer to discover and get control of the parts of their bodies that they can't easily see. They actually can't relate to their entire body as something that belongs to them. It takes them a long time to become cognizant and aware that they have a head, two arms, two legs, etc., and that all of these parts are connected into one whole thing called their body and that they are responsible for it.

Because of this challenge to locate one's own body, severely autistic people need to find ways to assure themselves that they have a body and that they are in their bodies. Moreover, they need to find ways to simulate the experience of boundaries and home that most people have automatically. Now we are starting to understand that the issue of having a sense of security and boundaries might have to be artfully or artificially constructed by the person with strong autistic perception. Sometimes severely autistic people will do some really strange things that seem incomprehensible to most people. But the answer may sometimes be found in their search for a boundary, some clue that reassures them that they are really there.

At the same time, we should understand repetitive motions as a means for continually touching base with a boundary. To do something over and over is to simulate boundaries within which an autistic person can create some kind of comfort zone for themselves. It might be the closest they can come to experiencing themselves as themselves. For these reasons, teachers of severely autistic children should understand their goals in terms of finding repetitive routines that entail functional skills as well as a sense of well-being.

Ironically, what teachers of severely autistic children need most is the ability to see themselves through the eyes of the autistic children they are teaching. This has been impossible. But, it should be quite clear by now that an understanding of social and computer thinking along with the functions of each may provide the insight necessary to connect with severely autistic children in meaningful ways.

Teaching and interacting with high-functioning autistic people

Autism is absolutely fascinating. High-functioning autism represents more social thinking. Teaching these people will be a different experience than teaching severely autistic people. These people will be much more adept at social life. But, the challenges they face will still be rooted in the phenomena we just covered in our discussion of severely autistic people. In other words, now we can imagine that the circle of light is quite a bit larger.

What is perhaps most difficult at this point is to draw a line between severe autism and high-functioning autism. I would like to propose a starting point. We could talk all day long about the differences in language use or the ability to learn social skills. But, one good way to differentiate between severe autism and high-functioning autism might be to say that a person is high-functioning when they care what other people think about them. After introducing the pictures in the first chapter, I would be the first person to say that there is a range of autistic perception. On the one hand, it is confusing because that implies that there is a range of severe autism and a range of high-functioning autism. And who has the right to draw a line between the two? But, for the sake of being practical I would say there is something utterly critical about a person being able to care what other people think about them. To have a social conscience is the hallmark of a high-functioning person because this singular ability is the dividing line between a person being able to motivate themselves to learn social skills and a person who simply does not care.

In high-functioning autism we begin to find people who are aware of the fact that they are autistic. We find people who recognize that they are different than other people. Let me point out quickly that some people can start out their lives as severely autistic people and can grow into high-functioning perception in their adolescence. Varying degrees of normalization can continue on into adulthood from any starting point in the range of autistic perception. This should give parents and teachers much hope and motivation for the emotional support of their autistic children. So, teachers need to be vigilant and always looking for signs that a social conscience is dawning inside the mind of any given autistic child.

At this point, everything that was said about severely autistic children above still applies. However, now we have a new sense of urgency because we are faced with a person whose potential to function in social life is far less limited. Furthermore, the ability of such a person to engage in social life will probably exist in direct proportion to the amount of social support they have from compassionate, understanding people around them.

In a pragmatic sense, the limits of a high-functioning autistic person are defined by their social surroundings. It is up to us to decide what kind of activity ensures safety and comfort for the high-functioning person as well as for those around that person. It is also up to us to give that person enough room to grow so that we can see what they are capable of achieving.

First, we need to understand that they will likely excel at some kind of activity that requires If-Then thinking. For example, they might enjoy something mechanical. If you teach a high-functioning person how to fix bicycles, you might have the most dependable and excellent bicycle mechanic you ever wanted. Everything about mechanics is rooted in If-Then rules. There is very little about bicycle mechanics that is explicitly social or interactive. All of the ways and means of bicycle mechanics can be described in terms of If-Then rules for action.

That brings us to another important point. Since we know the importance of If-Then rules, teachers and parents should strive to communicate as much as possible in terms of If-Then rules for action. It might seem boring or repetitive to the teacher or the parent, but it is the best way to communicate with the high-functioning person.

At the same time, remember to use the third person as often as you like, because this will be accessible to the person. Putting this all together makes for a structured approach. We can build a systematic way to communicate with high-functioning people by understanding them and seeing the world through their eyes.

Sometimes high-functioning people will tend to blurt out things that might not be socially acceptable. When a high-functioning child meets a person with a wart on their nose, don't be surprised if they shout out, "That person has a wart on their nose." The best way to use this as an opportunity to teach social skills is to combine some of the strategies we have been discussing. Respond with a combination of If-Then rules for action, and refer to the person in the third person.

For example, a teacher or parent might say, "Listen to me, Jimmy: if Jimmy meets someone, then Jimmy can't say what Jimmy thinks about that person; if Jimmy says what Jimmy thinks, then Jimmy might hurt their feelings; if Jimmy hurts their feelings, then Jimmy might make them sad." It will always require much patience to teach social skills to a high-functioning person. But the promise of some normalization makes it a worthwhile venture.

Since high-functioning people have relatively low social thinking they will also have trouble learning the meaning of shame, embarrassment, and humiliation. Here again, much patience is required. The catch is that the high-functioning person will have the ability to care about what other people are thinking. They may not ever master the social graces, but they will likely care enough to make conscientious efforts. With the right support this could be a rewarding experience for all concerned.

High-functioning people will tend to be very focused with whatever is occupying their attention. One of the most important things for a teacher is to make sure they are paying attention. A good teacher will not take offense at this. They will understand that autistic perception is repetitive, persevering perception, so we can expect a high-functioning person to stare or become hyper-focused. Sometimes, just calling their name a little more loudly is all that is required to get their attention. At the same time, this does not have to be done with urgency or emotion.

In fact, communicating with the high-functioning autistic person may be done more successfully with a monotone delivery. The teacher might just cup their hands to amplify their voice a little and say, "Jimmy. It is time for Jimmy to pay attention now, it is time for Jimmy to pay attention now." Then direction can be given and received with much less difficulty. The teacher might even use a paper towel roll to do this.

A patient teacher with a monotone, emotionless delivery, who understands the importance of repetitive routines, and who can speak in the third person to the high-functioning person, might find themselves able to draw out the best in that person in a very practical way.

Teaching and interacting with slightly autistic people

Like Alice said, things are getting curiouser and curiouser. At least we know what to look for when we are identifying and helping a person who is severely autistic. At least we can know that our patience may be rewarded when dealing with a high-functioning person. But, the slightly autistic person presents another level of mystery all together. Let's consider some clues to look for, and let's say that a preponderance of these clues might encourage significant others to wonder if they have a candidate for slightly autistic perception in their midst. In this section the focus is on people with high-level slightly autistic perception (see Figure 1.5).

First of all, a person with high-level slightly autistic perception will probably never be diagnosed as autistic. However, they might eventually become ripe candidates for any of a host of labels, such as obsessive-compulsive disorder, anxiety disorder, agoraphobia, depression, and so on. They might suffer from repeated earaches as children. They might have problems with authority as adults. They might have very smooth or fair skin. They might suffer from allergies. This person is different than everybody else. They are decidedly not normal. Their friends and family will recognize it, but their teachers may not be able to put their finger on it. And one fine day the slightly autistic person might even recognize it themselves.

It's one thing for a parent to have to hear "Your child is autistic" or "There is a good chance your child is high-functioning autistic." But it is quite another thing for a parent to have to hear "There is something wrong with your child, but I don't have any idea what it is." Maybe this is the hallmark of the slightly autistic person. They are noticeably different, but it is hard to say exactly why or how this person is different. They march to the beat of a different drummer!

They may be recognized as gifted or talented. But they might not have a strong desire to participate in normal social life. They may be a behavior problem in school because they never fully appreciate the importance of social rules. But they might be as quiet as a churchmouse and painfully shy.

They might be really good in one subject at school, and really bad at another. But they might be really good at something that is never taught in school, and they might end up dropping out of school.

They might have an unusual talent or skill in some area of life and be recognized as having achieved some high level of mastery. But they might be unable to commit to anyone or anything.

They might be a neat freak or a clean freak who insists on being meticulously organized. But they might live in squalor, preferring to wear the same clothes over and over again.

They might become a computer engineer capable of commanding six-figure salaries, which they collect as they hop from one job to another. But, they might end up homeless, preferring to travel the same interstate route over and over and over again.

Keep in mind, we are really addressing a range of autistic perception that is not diagnosable in current clinical terms. Within this range there will be lesser to stronger autistic perception as well. Stronger versions of slight autism might begin to be qualified as Asperger's syndrome. These people will have some kind of challenge participating in social organizations as well as some kind of challenge communicating. For example, as slightly autistic perception gets stronger we might see a person who has trouble with names and proper nouns. A person who is slightly autistic may tend to have trouble saying and pronouncing names. But, they may tend to enjoy making up nicknames. And they may have a tendency to hesitate in normal speech for unnatural periods of time, or to stammer or stutter when speaking in public.

Parents and teachers should be on the lookout for these and any other signs indicating a person who is standing on the outside looking in on the normal world. These people will manifest their predilection for repetitive behaviors in the form of long hours practicing or studying their favorite pursuits. This leads to mastery. This also leads away from the normal social world.

The single best way to communicate with a person like this is to recognize them for what they are. This person will respond to an understanding approach. They need to be told that they are different. They need to be told that they are special. They also need to be taught the importance of finding strategies for functioning and surviving in the world. This person needs to be held responsible for their actions and they need to have a strong social support system. Ideally, they would be in the habit of consulting with someone they respect before making important life decisions.

Of course, this won't come easy, because this person will always be striking out on their own. They are smart enough and aloof enough to make something of their differences. This person needs constant challenge and constant social support. In an ideal world they would have a therapist they can always consult regarding personal and social issues. But parents and teachers also need to be firm regarding the need to communicate well with others, to build positive relationships, and always to seek out help with these issues.

It is important not to be condescending with these people. It is also important for these people to learn not to be condescending with others. With adults, if this person loves you, they will be loyal and selfless to a fault. But if you do not inspire this person, they won't be around for long. Give them an anchor in the social world, and they might give you the best they have to give.

Sometimes people who are high on the computer have trouble with the basics. A person who is slightly autistic, and not diagnosable, may nevertheless have tremendous difficulty with the basics in any setting. This applies to a new subject in school, or a new job. It is possible that with effort and enthusiasm that same person will reach intermediate levels of performance and actually excel into advanced levels of performance with ease.

They may respond well to a challenge. One way to get them motivated might be to say, "Lots of people have trouble with this, I guess I couldn't expect you to do it either – what do you think?" instead of saying, "You had better do this or else."

Discipline is an interactive, social concept and it can be a strange experience for parents and teachers to see a slightly autistic child not responding in normal ways to discipline. At the same time, this could be the perfect child who is seen and not heard. Furthermore, this person could achieve much self-discipline and display will-power and focus beyond normal appearances. This person will tend to be characterized as a person of extremes who sees the world in exaggerated terms. Parents and teachers should remember that the normal social world will not be a place of much excitement or interest for these people. For these reasons, slightly autistic people will be motivated by appeals to higher loyalties and loftier goals.

Conclusion

From a social psychological point of view, we can expect to find stressful reactions to anything that strikes us as not normal. So, autism continually challenges our assumptions of normalcy, and this becomes very stressful for families of autism. Maybe if we could loosen our assumptions of normalcy a little bit, we might also be able to free ourselves from much of the stress associated with autism. In a world that understands autism we will be able to embrace the virtues and vicissitudes of autistic perception and behavior, and adjust our reactions accordingly.

It is possible that most of the stress of dealing with autism lies in our normal perception being unable to understand it. We can't wait any longer for the medical model to explain autistic perception and behavior to us. But ideas like this simple model of social and computer thinking may shed enough light on autistic perception that we can melt the ice of our apprehensions and stress enough to deal with autistic people calmly and confidently.

In other words, it's what you assume is normal that's driving you crazy. If you lived in a world where autism was considered normal, you would not experience the same level of fear, stress, and apprehension currently experienced. If you lived in a world where autism was understood, you would even be proud to take care of a person with autism.

We tend to focus too much on normalcy as the gold standard for meaningful experience. Every human has social and computer thinking and every human is therefore an interactive creature to one extent or another. The trick is to recognize this and understand each human being on his or her own particular terms. Even a person with severe autism registers the world around them and has likes and dislikes.

But in a worldview controlled by the medical model anything that is not normal is automatically framed in a deficit approach. People with autism should not be treated as broken people who need to be fixed. They represent the miracle of life in their own particular way. Maybe people with autism will eventually challenge the normal world to reexamine its own rigid standards for acceptance and meaning.

People in the normal world should not be offended by autism and should not be on the defensive when it comes to interacting with autistic people. People with autism are capable of sharing their own perception in ways that can be illuminating, humorous, and insightful. People with autism are capable of exhibiting compassion and loyalty. In short, they are whatever we can help them to be, given their own levels of social and computer thinking.

On the one hand, if an autistic person speaks in a robotic tone, or walks on their tip-toes, this may seem strange to a normal person. But as we begin to understand autism it will become easier and easier for us to deal with autistic people. Given that we have some understanding, then we are in a position patiently and compassionately to address the needs of such people in a supportive way. Interestingly, the stronger a person's autistic perception, the more they will want to be left alone. So, it's not as if people with strong autistic perception will ever be intrusive or demanding in terms of their social expectations. That only applies to normal people in the normal world!

If we can sidestep our assumptions of normalcy and apprehend an easy way of understanding autism, then we will be able to begin making realistic assessments of autism. Whether we are subscribing to normal common sense or normal science, it is difficult to understand autism from a normal point of view. But if we are able somehow to see the world through the eyes of a person with autism, then we will surely arrive at a new appreciation for people with autism, for our society at large, and for ourselves.

Index

CPSIA information can be obtained at www.ICGtesting.com
Printed in the USA
BVOW040016270911

272044BV00006B/3/P